Chin Sheng Yang

Throughout His Whole Life had the Boy Been Struggling from Taiwan to America

novum ▟ premium

This book is also available as e-book.

www.novumpublishing.com

© 2019 novum publishing

ISBN 978-1-64268-047-8
Editing: Karen Simmering
Cover photos: Kontur-vid,
Gstudioimagen | Dreamstime.com
Cover design, layout & typesetting:
novum publishing
Internal illustrations: Chin Sheng Yang

The images provided by the author
have been printed in the highest
possible quality.

www.novumpublishing.com

Contents

Preface

This story is about a child who was adopted when he was a baby. But the boy didn't know he was adopted until he was 13 years old. During grade school, after school hours and on weekends, he helped the family water vegetables in the suburbs, and in the streets he peddled popsicles, peanut candy, egg cakes, fried dough sticks, and fried tofu.

During the summer vacation of junior high school, this boy worked as a coolie, carrying gravel, sand and bricks at job sites. Because he doubled his efforts in studying, within three years, his school scores went from almost the lowest in the first year of junior high to the top scores in the third year; and finally the teacher appointed him a class monitor.

In 1950, considering the family's poor economic condition and being incapable of attaining continuing education, the boy made a bet with his adoptive mother: if he couldn't pass the entrance examination of the Taipei Institute of Technology (TIT), then he should become an apprentice, making money to support the family. So his mother borrowed the entrance examination fee for him from the neighbors, and fortunately, he passed the exam to get into that school.

After having graduated from the five-year institute, he spent six years working for three factories in Taiwan. Since he had excellent grades, he applied for and obtained a full scholarship from a graduate school in the United States.

17

After coming to the United States and finding a part-time job, he sent back the borrowed money to the neighbors in Taiwan. Without any money, he struggled alone in the United States. In order to enter the top ten schools in the U.S., he gave up his scholarship and worked in restaurants and farms to achieve financial independence.

When he was studying at the University of California at Los Angeles, he would attend class or assist the professor with research in the radiation lab in the mornings. Then in the afternoon he worked for the Payne Heater Company off campus. In the evening he worked as a salad man in a restaurant. During summer vacations he worked on a farm.

In 1964, he obtained admission to the University of Southern California (USC) for a master's degree in mechanical engineering. During that time he worked full-time in an engineering company, and spent the nights studying as a full-time student.

In 1967, after getting a master's degree from USC, he was employed by Boeing in Seattle, Washington. While he was employed there, Boeing paid his tuition to pursue a PhD at the University of Washington in Seattle.

For the three years that he worked at Boeing, he considered his job to be his main priority, while his studies were secondary. When he decided to work for the Bechtel Power Company in San Francisco, he was choosing to develop his career instead of pursuing a doctoral degree.

During his period of employment at Bechtel, he began to invest in real estate, using money he saved from his wages.

In 1978, after eight years at the company, he was promoted to an engineering specialist and unit supervisor, praised in the Bechtel company magazine published yearly, and also listed in the yearbook of "Who's Who Worldwide."

After 17 years at Bechtel, the company wanted to send him to New Jersey to work at the nuclear power plant for two years. However, feeling that he needed to stay in the Bay Area to manage his real estate investments, he refused. He found a job in the Caesar Engineering Company in Oakland, on the other side of San Francisco. Currently he is semi-retired. Part of the time, based on his many years of experience with real estate management and maintenance, he has been acting as a consultant in a friend's company. The rest of his time he spends traveling around the world.

The book, "Throughout his whole life had a boy been struggling from Taiwan to America, to pursuit the freedom, democrat, human right, morality, and wealth," was not only written as a memoir, but also to hopefully provide hope and a reference for others. His life's work and philosophy has been to overcome poverty and to rise from adversity to a prosperous and successful life. One should have been suffered by adversity as if one had experienced it oneself to really being capable of acquainted with the real meaning of this book.

Chin Sheng Yang
California, U.S.A.
February 25, 2019

1 Childhood

1.1 The hardship of the farmer's life

This story starts in 1935, on a small island called Taiwan or Formosa the Republic of China (ROC), or Free China, adjacent to the east of China, the north of Philippines, and the southwest of Japan and Korea. About 50 minutes south of Taipei, there was a small, secluded village called New Village, and in this village lived a family named Hsu.

At the beginning of the 20 century, because the Hsu family had only one daughter and no son, they adopted a boy from the Chiu family, who lived in a nearby village, to carry on the Hsu name. Because they later gave birth to two boys, the family finally consisted of one biological sister, two biological brothers, and one adopted boy.

Later, the adopted boy married and had three sons and three daughters. They were what is called tenant farmers, so every year they paid rent or a certain amount of paddy to the landlord.

At that time, due to the underdevelopment of agriculture, the lagging agricultural technology, and annual natural disasters, they had almost no harvest. Even so, they had to pay yearly rent on the paddy; and what with overwork and undernourishment, the whole family had fallen ill.

A fourth boy was born to the unhealthy mother but died in a few months. When a fifth child was born, the family was afraid they could not afford to raise it; therefore, they put the boy up for adoption at a couple of weeks of age. This was not an uncommon practice for families who could not afford to raise their children.

1.2 The adoption of the boy

There was a town called Taoyuan, located about 30 miles south of Taipei. In an alley in this town there were 14 families, including the Yang family, who lived in a dirt-bamboo hut. The walls were built out of woven bamboo and covered with a mix of red mud, seaweed and straw; the roof was only laid with thin black tiles and no ceilings, and the floor was constructed not with concrete but clay. On rainy days, water would drip directly onto the clay floor, making it a slippery mess. Such shabby bungalows were rare in the town, being more common in the countryside.

This is where the adopted boy lived. When he was 13 years old, he realized he was adopted. Later, when he came back to Taiwan from America to visit the Hsu family, he found out that the sixth brother had died early, as the fourth brother did. That meant that two babies had died only months after their births. The adopted boy stood in fifth position among the brothers.

Logically guessing, if the fifth boy had not been adopted, he most likely would not have survived.

2 Boyhood

2.1 Crying to have a tricycle

When the boy was five years old, his adoptive father, who loved him very much, took him to Taipei to see his eldest uncle. As they walked near Taipei's train station, they passed a store that sold adult bicycles and children's tricycles.

The adoptive father took him into the store to take a look. He had no intention of buying a tricycle for the boy. But the boy had long wanted to have a tricycle. When they left the store, he began to cry.

The adoptive father told him they would go back to the store and buy a tricycle, and the boy immediately stopped crying. However, when they got to the store, the adoptive father realized that a tricycle would cost the equivalent of half a month's wages, and they turned to leave the store.

When the boy began to cry again, the adoptive father finally had no choice, and bought him a tricycle. This showed how much his adoptive father loved him.

2.2 Attending the sworn sisters' banquet of the adoptive mother

Whenever the adoptive mother attended the sworn sister banquet, she always took him with her. When he attended these parties he enjoyed the sumptuous meals. But he had never seen any other sisters taking their children to the dinner party.

The adoptive mother had another way to love him: according to the Taiwanese custom, every year there were several festivals to worship the gods. After the worship of the ritual, she always made sure that the sacrificial offerings of chicken legs were left for him to eat.

During World War II, food was regulated and allocated by the government. Once a month, every Taiwanese family had to queue up to buy their rations of pork and bean cake from the market.

2.3 A low-flying airplane shooting a machine gun

In the summer of 1942, the adoptive parents were hired at the nearby Pu Xin military airfield as a plasterer and a cook, respectively. They also took that boy to the temporarily built bungalow for workers, and stayed together for several weeks.

One early morning, when the sun had just risen, nobody was walking outside, and the boy was playing by himself at the nearby riverside. Suddenly, an American B-39 flew by, swooping down to several hundred meters above the ground. The airplane looked like the front of a locomotive with wings. It was flying at about three hundred meters above the ground, straight at him. He was so scared that he raced immediately back home.

The airplane fired its machine guns, but no bullet hit him. Most likely the reasons he escaped were because he swerved left and right as he ran, their technology was not good enough to hit such a small moving target, he got quickly to the workers' bungalows, and probably the gunmen only wanted to frighten him.

3 The primary school

A 3.5 years under Japanese rule Spring-Sun Primary School ... From Sections 3.1 to 3.4

3.1 The first year of elementary school ... Japanese rule

3.1.1 The teacher who loved the boy's singing

During the Japanese era, under the education system in Taiwan, children were expected to begin school at the age of seven full or eight nominal years. During spring-time, the boy, who was just over seven years old, entered the first year of Spring-Sun Elementary School (now East-Gate Elementary School).

On the first day of school, the adoptive mother and the boy, both in bare feet, walked for more than 20 minutes to arrive at the school.

Entering a classroom, the mother found his designated seat, then hurried away from the classroom and went home.

At that time, Taoyuan only had two elementary schools where Taiwanese children could study. Besides the school he attended in the eastern outskirts, there was another school in the city center called Wuling Elementary School (now Taoyuan Elementary School).

That boy's teacher was a woman who was also a music teacher. When the class stood up to sing, he sang loudly and elegantly. Later the teacher asked him to sing alone, apparently liking his singing very much. She had a son of the same age as that boy, but they were in different classes. The teacher often invited that boy to go to her house to play with her son.

3.1.2 Listening to the radio for gymnastics

During the summer, in order to keep all the students healthy, the school requested that every student went to the school playground at six o'clock in the morning, and they followed the music of the radio for gymnastics.

After gymnastics, each student went home to have breakfast, and then returned to school for their classes. Sometimes instead of doing gymnastics, the teachers would take their students to climb the nearby Shrine Hill (now Tiger Head Hill).

3.2 The second year of elementary school ... Japanese rule

3.2.1 On the track of the athletic field the whole class crawled

That year, that boy's teacher was a retired soldier. When he was angry with the class, he punished the students by making them crawl on their elbows and knees for two laps on the athletic field.

Most of the students ended up with bleeding elbows or knees after this punishment, but the left knee of the boy was injured so badly that even now his knee will occasionally still swell and ache.

3.2.2 Accidental head injury requiring five stitches

Because at that time the family had no refrigerator, left-overs were covered and left on the table for the next meal. Under each leg of the ancient dining table was a pottery tray filled with water so that ants would not climb up to eat the reserved food.

One day, when the boy and his second-eldest sister were chasing each other around the table, he accidentally fell and cut his head on the pottery tray. Seeing the bleeding, his adoptive mother circled his waist with her right hand

and used her left to put pressure on the wound. His sister took his feet and the mother and sister carried him to the nearby hospital, where he received five stitches on his scalp.

3.3 The third year of elementary school …
   Japanese rule

3.3.1 In order to water vegetables,
   the boy dropped into the creek

Since the third grade, after class and Sundays, the boy assisted his adoptive mother with irrigating vegetable fields in the suburbs.

One of his strongest memories is the time that he fell into the brook. He assisted his adoptive mother in watering vegetable gardens in the suburbs until she decided that he was old enough to do the job by himself. He was always careful not to arrive at the vegetable gardens too late, since that would mean he had to finish in the dark.

In the bushes behind the vegetable garden there was a bamboo grove, and next to the grove was a brook. When the sun was setting, the water in the brook would flash with the reflecting light in black and white bursts. Therefore, after sunset, for a little boy passing the terrible flashing water, the rustling bamboo and the shaking jungle was a frightening ordeal.

At that time, they used a tin bucket to collect water from the small brook at the bottom of the sloped road. The bucket of water was carried by hand to the top of the sloped road and then down to the vegetable field.

This was not an easy job for a small boy. The watering bucket was too big for him to easily lift, but too small to carry a useful amount of water. If he filled the bucket too much the water would overflow, but if he didn't fill it enough, he had to make more trips and he got very tired. After a while, he was so tired that the water overflowed more, and eventually the water overflowed so much that the slope became slick. Soon the road was such a slippery mess that he slid into the creek.

At that time he couldn't swim yet. Fortunately the water was only up to his neck, so he was able by floundering around with his hands and feet to get himself out, soaking wet and exhausted. The sun was just going down behind the hill, and nobody was around, so he took off his clothes, wrung them out and put them back on.

3.3.2 Cutting weeds for stacking and drying to become fertilizer

Because there was virtually no sports equipment at the school, the students' only options were to run on the track, listen to the radio to do gymnastics, or practice the long jump and high jump.

During wartime, instead of sports, the students planted oil trees and removed weeds. The seeds of the oil tree could be refined into airplane oil, while the weeds could be stacked, dried and used as fertilizer.

3.3.3 Watching the rice harvest in the countryside

One summer, his classmate Yang invited several classmates to visit his father's farm and see the rice harvest. At lunch, all of the students were treated with chicken, pork, vegetables and dry rice.

During World War II, this delicious lunch only could be afforded by farmers. Most people were only able to get porridge with shredded sweet potatoes, and the allocated pork.

3.3.4 The first time seeing a beautiful private garden

In the third grade, there was a teacher surnamed Yao who taught the students to sing at lunchtime. He usually allowed the students to nap on their desks after lunch for five minutes, and then began their singing lesson.

Every time after the students sang, the teacher always had the boy stand and sing a solo. One day, he asked the boy to come home with him to get rid of the weeds in the rear garden.

This garden was a rectangular style: there were three small rock mounds each about twelve feet high, at the left, center and right sides, respectively. On each mountain was planted many species of Japanese potted plants, decorated with ceramic statues of people, birds, horses, cows, arch bridges, and pavilions, and each mound had a paved cement hallway in front of it.

At the foot of the mounds were brooks flowing from left, center and right. The water flowed into a pipe buried underneath the cement hallway and then into the gourd-shaped pond in the garden center.

There was a fountain at the center of the pond surrounded by lawns and colorful flowers; water was sprayed directly up for about a meter, and then spread back to the pond.

The boy had never seen such a beautiful and elegant garden. He eradicated all the weeds and cleaned the dirt from the path before going home to tell his family about the most beautiful garden he'd ever seen. His grandma told him that the teacher came from one of the finest local noble families. The huge sum of money that had been used to build the garden could have built a house, and the gap between rich and poor families was really too big.

3.3.5 Picking up withered branches from the mountain for cooking material

Coal or wood was usually used for cooking, but during the Second World War, coal couldn't be used anymore, since it was needed for battleships.

Every family tried to find fuel substitutes to save money. The boy and the daughter of the family who ran the Chinese medicine shop, who was five years older than him, went together to the mountain to gather withered branches from the ground for kindling.

At about six o'clock in the morning, each person carried one stick. Half an hour after arriving at the foot of the mountain, they were walking slowly toward the top of the mountain picking up the withered branches from the ground under the trees.

When they arrived at the top, each person had two small bundles of withered tree branches, using each end of stick inserted into each bundle, put the center of each stick on each shoulder, and then carried it back home.

This was his first trip to the mountain. He climbed up so high that he could view the whole city of Taoyuan, and felt like his body was floating in the sky.

3.3.6 Grinding rice to making the festival cakes

In Taiwan there were four festivals every year: New Year Day, Poet Festival, July Ghost Day, and Mid-Autumn Festival. Grinding rice to make the rice cakes for worship was an important part of the festival, and the boy was always responsible for this job.

The grinding process was as follows: the grandmother mixed glutinous rice with water and poured a spoon of this rice-water into the small hole in the upper stone wheel. The boy used both hands to grasp the ends of the grinding bar handle and moved it in a circular direction. When the stone wheel was moved one circle, with one spoonful of the rice-water, then the rice pulp would flow from the lower stone wheel through a hole and into a tin bucket. The boy found this a relaxing job. He could grind for hours and never get tired.

3.4 Fourth year of elementary school ... Japanese rule

3.4.1 The suffering of World War II in Taiwan

World War II was a terrible time. The school required all the students to use their spare time doing the following tasks:

1) Mowing weeds and stacking them in the corner of the athletic field to dry for fertilizer;

2) Collecting scrap metal for the manufacture of weapons; and

3) Growing oil-seed trees for the refining of aircraft fuel.

Before the end of the Second World War, Japan had conquered these islands and countries in Southeast Asia: Manila, Ishmael Islands, Yangon, Indonesia, Myanmar, Mindoro, and so on. Whenever the Japanese conquered a place, all the students in the school were required to hold the Japanese flag, sing Japanese victory songs, and march on the streets.

After the parade, they would get a piece of glutinous cake. Even at night the lighted-candle lanterns were used to celebrate the war victory. The lanterns could be bought from the shop, but were also made by the students themselves. The boy's lantern was made by himself.

3.4.2 Evacuating to the countryside to escape bombing

In order to reduce injuries during air raids, the government asked people to observe the following provisions:

1) Each person had to have a defense head cloth, stuffed with cotton and long enough to cover the shoulders. Students would carry these to school every day.

2) Air raid trenches had to be dug in the living room of each family.

3) Each family's windows had to be cover with paper so that fragments wouldn't hurt people in the event of an explosion.

4) After 10 o'clock in the evening, all lights must be extinguished, with no light leakage.

The government required every family to evacuate to the suburbs to escape the bombing in the city.

The boy and his grandmother moved to a rural area, about an hour's walk away from the city. The other family members remained in the city to make money for living.

In the evacuation period, he learned how to cook from his grandmother. When the air raid bombarded the Taoyuan area, the damage was less than in other big cities, but in the area near the Pacific Ocean coast, the Pu Xin military airport was bombed far more heavily and miserably.

3.4.3 At Chiayi train station to escape the bombing unscathed

One day when his adoptive father brought the boy to buy some cheap daily necessities in the south, the air raid bombed the Chiayi railroad station. They were lucky;

they had left the train station five minutes before the bombing and so were unscathed.

Having escaped without injury, they canceled their plans, quickly returned to the station, and took the next north-bound train home.

3.4.4 Japan surrenders unconditionally

On August 15, 1945, the Japanese Emperor declared unconditional surrender: World War II had ended, the Japanese rule of Taiwan for 50 years was also over, and Taiwan was free. All the people on the island celebrated the termination of colonial rule.

The day of October 25 was designated as the day that Taiwan gained independence from Japan. The people who had evacuated to the countryside all moved back to the city where they'd lived before. The boy carried his aunt, who was heavier than himself, on his back for more than an hour to return to their original home.

B Three years under the Chinese controlled era East-Gate Primary School … From Sections 3.5 to 3.7

3.5 The fourth year primary school … Chinese rule

3.5.1 The difference between two educational systems

During the era of Japanese rule, the school started in the spring. In the Republic of China era, it began in the fall. Students at the school were forced to speak Japanese, but at home the boy and his family still spoke Taiwanese. It was no wonder that his Japanese school grades were so poor. It was so strange that in the Japanese school his school ranking was always third from the bottom, but in the Chinese school his ranking was always third from the top.

After the independence of Taiwan, due to the language change from Japanese to Chinese, his school record went from bad to good. When he was comfortable with the language, he became more interested in his studies, kept up more with his school work, and his grades naturally became excellent.

3.5.2 The hawkers selling vegetables

During the summer vacation, to earn some money, his adoptive mother sent the boy out to sell the vegetables she'd grown. She placed only one kind of vegetable in the handbasket to give to him to sell on the street. But he did not dare to try peddling, so he went to sit on the entrance steps of the temple to sell vegetables.

When worshipers came up the stone temple steps, he would ask them whether they wanted to buy some vegetables. After he had been sitting there about two hours, the vegetables began to wither, so he took the whole basket of unsold vegetables home. The non-withered vegetables were still able to be cooked for eating. He only tried to sell vegetables once, since they wilted too quickly in the hot summer.

3.6 The fifth year primary school ... Chinese rule

3.6.1 Sleeping unknowingly with a dead person all night

His adoptive father's mother often stayed with her three sons in Taipei. One time when she was suffering from a serious illness, the eldest son asked the third son, the boy's adoptive father, to take her in for a while.

Because the third son had filial piety, he agreed to his brother's request, bringing her back to Taoyuan to nurse her.

The three brothers opened a grocery store, and lived together in the back of store. The fourth brother, who did the carpentry work, lived in another place. The boy called the grandma in Taipei "Taipei grandma," while the other was known as "Taoyuan grandma."

In the living room, there was an extra-large bed, a wooden rectangle about 4 meters wide by 3 meters long, spread with a sheet of straw linen, and occupying roughly one-third of the living room space. This bed could accommodate up to five or six people to sleep, but at this time only that boy and his "Taipei grandma" slept in the big bed.

The Taipei grandma had been in Taoyuan about two weeks. One afternoon when the boy came home from school, his adoptive mother told him not to sleep in that bed again, because his Taipei grandma had passed away last night. He was surprised, and incredulous. He had slept in a bed for a night with the dead grandma and didn't know she was dead. All of the relatives from Taipei came to Taoyuan to attend the funeral.

3.6.2 Participating in after-school study class

At the beginning of the sixth grade, the students were divided into two categories: the continuing school class and the employment class. After the regular class, the continuing school class, which the boy was assigned to, spent two more hours to prepare for the junior high school entrance examination. Between two hours of after-class study, there was a fifteen-minute break for a dodge ball game.

3.6.3 Self-taught to swim and nearly drowned

On a hot summer day, after school, the boy went to swim in the river with his classmates. About a 30-minute walk from the school there was a hill called "Shrine Hill" (now known as " Tiger Head Mountain Park"). Beneath the cliff, a river flowed along the hillside from the north to the south. This was the first time he went swimming, and no one had taught him how. He watched the other students, stripped off his shirt, and then walked slowly from the beach into the water.

At first he learned frog-style swimming because that was what his classmates were doing. In the shallow chest-deep water, he swam along the shore back and forth for five minutes, and then went back to the shore. An hour later he learned the backstroke and treading water. But when he stood straight up to test the water's depth, he discovered that his feet couldn't touch the bottom of river because the water was too deep. Panicking and feeling like he was drowning, he instinctively kicked with his left foot to the left side, floundering and swallowing a lot of water, until he gradually made his way back to the shore.

After that he hurried away from the river without saying goodbye to his classmates, got dressed quietly, and went back home alone. He was so relieved that he hadn't drowned that he felt as if he'd escaped from the gates of hell. After that incident, he did not try to swim again for a very long time.

3.6.4 A hawker selling popsicles

In summer, the boy began to peddle popsicles on the street. At that time, milk was not a common everyday drink for most people. Only infants who couldn't be fed by human milk from mothers could drink milk. Hence, instead of making "milk popsicles," the stores could only use water to make "ice popsicles."

He did so well that as soon as he went out with the cooler on his chest, people would run to him to buy popsicles. The weather was so hot that everyone felt too lazy to go to the store to buy them. The boy used the Taiwanese language while peddling, but Mandarin was never heard to be used for selling popsicles.

Selling popsicles was much easier than selling vegetables. He not only knew how to call out loud, but this time he also dared to asked passersby whether they wanted to buy. The popsicles had to be sold out within a certain amount of time, or they would melt. When they looked like they were beginning to melt, he rushed home to let his adoptive mother deal with it. It was a much simpler solution to let the popsicles melt in someone's stomach.

3.6.5 Watching the last five minutes of the opera for entertainment

During primary school, the boy's biggest entertainment was watching the last five minutes of the opera. Taiwanese opera was almost the same in costume as the Peking opera, but done in a different language for the singing and acting. During the year of 1947, there was only one theatre in Taoyuan town, and it only showed black and white films and the opera.

In addition to the enjoyment of the Taiwanese opera, he made three different types of toys for his own amusement: 1) the rubber band pistol, 2) the bamboo air gun, and 3) the wooden top.

The material to make these toys could be obtained from nearby bushes in his adoptive mother's vegetable field.

3.7 The six-year primary school ... Chinese rule

3.7.1 As a sprint and long-jump contestant representing the school at the county athletic meeting

When the boy was in the sixth grade of elementary school, he was selected as a contestant representing the school at the Taoyuan town (now Taoyuan County) athletic meeting. This county game was held at the Taoyuan agricultural vocational high school (now agricultural-industrial vocational high school). The Taoyuan Town Government (now Taoyuan County Government) organized such sports throughout the whole county.

From more than 100 students of the sixth graders, the PE teacher elected two students to participate. First, four kind of sports were tested: the high jump, long jump, triple jump and 100-meter race.

At the test results, the PE teacher selected him to participate in the long jump and 100-meter race, while another classmate participated in the high jump and triple jump. The other classmate was so tall that he was suitable for the high jump and triple jump. But the boy ran so fast that the PE teacher asked him to participate in the long jump and the 100-meter race.

On the day of the athletic meeting, both contestants hoped to get awards, but they didn't get any trophies. The reason for the failure was that they had been selected for the race too close to the race date, they didn't have enough time to practice, and they didn't get enough training.

3.7.2 Getting drinking water from an ancient well in the distance

The boy's house was located in the east side of the city. It was a long house between an alley and a big street. Of the six families that lived in the house, three took the alley as an exit, while the other three used the big street for an entrance.

His house was located beside the alley, which was more convenient for going in and out. The ancient well that was used for drinking water was about 30 meters behind the house; hence, it was really very inconvenient.

Water was usually stored in two large belly crocks covered with round wooden lids, which were placed in front of the kitchen range. Twice a week that boy went to pull water from the well behind the house. It took more than an hour to fill up the two crocks. When the well water was dirty or contaminated, that boy obtained the drinking water from the wells of the left neighbor or of the nearby temple. The economic conditions in the three families were so poor that they were unable to hire someone to clean the well.

3.7.3 After graduation, he was almost beaten by a group of graduates

In the summer of 1948, the boy graduated from East Gate Primary School. The graduation ceremony was held in the playground, where the students reluctantly sang a song of farewell. Then the teachers stood in front of the office with their graduating classes to take group photos.

Miss Wung, the directing teacher of the boy, brought two classes of graduates together for a photo. Now more than seven decades old, the photo has become faded and yellow, but you can still see that the students are barefoot, which is how they arrived at school every day.

After the graduation ceremony, the boy walked out of the school gate. He had walked about five minutes when a group of graduates that had been following him began to shout at him, obviously wanting to fight.

When he stopped, they quickly surrounded him. Why did they want to hit him? He didn't know. He hadn't fought with anybody during his six years at the primary school and he didn't remember any quarrels he'd had that would cause anyone to want to fight with him.

"Well, I'll fight with you," shouted one of the graduates. He apparently wanted to appear brave in front of his friends, who were egging him on.

In fact, the boy never fought or quarreled with this classmate, but he thought it might be impulsive and fun.

"If all of you were gentlemen, we could duel one by one," he told them calmly. "Groups fighting with a single man look like villains!"

1948 graduates from East Gate National Elementary School

"Okay! I'll duel with you," a volunteer said, encouraged by the other graduates.

The boy quickly grasped the volunteer's hands, pulled them forcefully, and spun him rapidly around three times before releasing him. The centrifugal force threw his opponent back three steps. He tottered, fell down, then finally got up and walked away.

The duel was over. After seeing the loser going home, no one dared to stand up to fight with him, and all the bystanders went home too.

3.7.4 Going to a different school district for the entrance exam of a junior industrial middle school

Located in the southern part of Taoyuan, about 30 minutes to the city of Xinzhu, there was a junior industrial middle school. In June of 1948, the boy attended the entrance examination for that school.

His adoptive mother brought him to her friend's house in Xinzhu to stay one night. The next morning, when he went to the exam place in the school, he saw a fighter jet, one that had flown in World War II, being displayed in the square between two buildings.

Very excited, he approached the airplane, studying the structures of its various parts, imagining having the opportunity to design one in the future. Twenty years later, he would actually work at Boeing, one of the largest aircraft manufacturing companies in the United States.

But he did not pass the exam, because at that time all the schools in Taiwan were not unified teaching; the different school districts taught with different textbooks.

In the meantime, Taiwan had just been recovering from Japanese rule for three years, and the Ministry of Education had not yet compiled a unified textbook for every school in Taiwan. The older brother of his classmate Guo had chosen this school for both classmates to take the examination, thinking that they could go together to school.

At that time, the academic capabilities of both were about the same level, but they both failed. It is generally believed that after graduating from industrial school, a student would have special skills and could easily find a job.

Because the test date of all Taipei schools had passed, both boys had to test at the local ordinary junior high school, Taoyuan Junior High School, and finally they passed the exam.

3.7.5 Hawker selling the peanut candy and the egg cake

About a block away from the boy's house, a middle-aged man made peanut candy and egg cake. He hired hawkers to sell these desserts for him on the streets. During the hot summer, it was best to sell the peanut candy as soon as possible, because it would quickly dissolve in the high temperatures, but the egg cake wasn't affect at all.

Fortunately, the peanut candy always sold out before they started to dissolve, and the egg cakes also had no problem being sold.

3.7.6 13 years later, the boy's identity was revealed

In September of 1948, a week before school began, the school stipulated that each new student should bring a household transcript to be registered.

So the adoptive mother gave the boy a household booklet and a seal in order to go to the town hall (now the city government) to apply for a copy of the household transcript.

When he received the household transcript from the clerk of the town hall, he was speechless. The parent column of the transcript indicated not only the names of his adoptive parents, but also his birth parents. He began to realize that what he thought were his parents were actually adoptive parents, and the uncle and the aunt his mother talked about were actually his biological parents.

He came home very calm and silent, being very careful not to show any emotion or sign that anything was wrong.

Without a word, he returned the household booklet and a seal of the adoptive father to his adoptive mother, and then walked away slowly.

Frequently his adoptive mother had often said to him that it was hard to raise a child, but the merits were very great. The biological mother might have 10 months of pregnancy and childbirth, but the adoptive parents carried the burden of child rearing a lifetime. They were the ones who cared for the children with the heart of love, providing food, clothing, living, and educational costs.

The adoptive mother used to say these things to the boy, but he didn't understand her meaning. When he was young, his uncle, actually his born father, often came to see him carrying with some fresh vegetables, because he was a farmer. He always talked to him in a soft and loving voice about interesting things. Obviously his uncle had actually been his biological father. Why would they keep this secret for 13 years? It is still a puzzle to him now!

4 Taoyuan Junior High School

4.1 The first year of junior high school

4.1.1 Taking the shoes off before entering the classroom

During the first day of school, at seven o'clock in the morning, the new students went to school, gathered in the playground, their teachers introduced the school profiles, and then both the new and old students attended the flag-raising ceremony.

After a speech by the principal, each class teacher brought his students to their classroom. In case of rain, the principal or teachers held a speech in the auditorium. This school was a little different from other schools in one way: before entering the classroom, shoes were removed.

In the Japanese colonial era, the school was called "Taoyuan home-economic girls' school." It only recruited female students. Hardwood floors were installed in classrooms, the auditorium and the hallways, and before entering the classroom, students would take off their shoes and leave them in boxes. When they came out of the classroom, they put their shoes on again.

There were three classes for the new students: Benevolence, Righteousness, and Courtesy. The boy was allocated to the Benevolence class.

50

4.1.2 Hawker selling fried dough sticks and fried tofu

When the boy was in the first grade of junior high school, a family located two blocks away from his house made fried dough sticks and fried tofu at home for hawkers to peddle on the street.

At four o'clock every morning, his adoptive mother went to help them cook the fried dough sticks and tofu to help support the family. She asked the boy to help sell these items at six o'clock in the morning, because these two fried goods were very popular breakfast foods.

When the sun was about to rise, whether sold out or not, he started to walk quickly back to the store to give back the unsold merchandise, because he was afraid the students of his own school would be embarrassed to see him selling something.

He was the youngest peddler on the street. For four years, from grade four to the first year of junior high school, he peddled a total of six items such as vegetables, popsicles, egg cakes, peanut cakes, deep-fried dough sticks and fried tofu. After his second year of junior high school, he did no more peddling.

4.1.3 Almost losing his voice from peddling

The boy once encountered the most feared situation during his peddling. He was selling the deep-fried dough sticks and fried tofu along an 80-metre-long street. On one side of the street, eucalyptus was planted every five meters; on the other side, there was a deep, wide ditch behind a row of houses. Every family had a wooden bridge that crossed the ditch to the road.

In the dark, cloudy and windy mornings, the clatter of leaves and the pounding of the water in the ditch created a terrible symphony. In order to reduce his fear and be heard above the noise, he raised his voice as he walked through the street. He yelled louder and louder, until finally he became hoarse and almost lost his voice.

"Give me two pieces of deep-fried dough sticks and three pieces of fried tofu," a customer wearing a sleeping robe called to him.

Several sales on that terrible street calmed down the fear of the adopted boy. At that time, three types of hawkers were hawking food on the streets at different times: morning hawkers, day vendors and evening hawkers. The daytime hawker had the longest selling time, the evening hawker second, and early morning hawker shortest.

4.1.4 228 events occurred in junior high school year

While he was in the first year of junior high school, 228 events that rocked the island took place. On February 28, 1949, after police shot a woman to death who was selling banned cigarettes in the streets of Taipei, residents of the whole island rebelled against the government.

At that time that boy was still small. He remembered that after the morning flag-raising ceremony, he took off his shoes to go into the classroom. He had just sat down when the teacher came in and asked the students to go home quickly.

Sure enough, not long after, he heard sporadic gunfire. His grandmother told him that outside was very messy, so he stayed at home the whole day without going out.

4.1.5 Being a cement worker in the high-rise buildings

In the summer vacation of junior high school, the adoptive father and his two apprentices worked in the big city of Taipei in a five-story office building. The top floor was to be renovated, but the adoptive father was only responsible for the cement portion of engineering.

One day at lunchtime, while the adoptive father and his two apprentices were eating in another room, the boy decided to learn how to paste a layer of cement on a red brick wall. So he picked up the tool and coated about a square meter of the wall. Coming back to the original work spot after lunch, his adoptive father saw the wall covered with an extra layer of coating about a square meter. The adoptive father was so angry that he immediately scraped away the extra part.

"If you do this kind of work, I needn't send you to school," he said in an angry tone to the boy.

The adoptive father really loved him and wanted to let him concentrate on his studying, hoping for him to be able to get ahead.

4.1.6 Reading English loudly facing the open window, lest it wake up the family

During the first year of junior high school, the boy began to study English. At home in the morning, in order to read English loudly without disturbing the still sleeping family, he put a desk next to the open window beside the street and recited his English texts loudly.

But the sound of his recitation could be heard by the people passing by on the street, even to the third house down, because every morning at 6 o'clock, the neighbor had to take two barrels of boiled peanut soup and almond tea to his store near the train station to sell, He was benefited by the early morning recitation with its standard pronunciation and clear voice for the speech contest and the advanced study in the U.S.A. in future.

4.2 The second year of junior high school

4.2.1 Producing the desire to study abroad by volunteering to stay in the classroom to review homework

From the first semester of the second year of junior high school, after the last session of daily class, that boy voluntarily stayed in the classroom one more hour, so that he could review that day's lessons or preview the next day's.

From then on, whenever his adoptive mother did not ask him to return early to water the vegetables, he would stay in the classroom to review his lessons. After staying several times in the classroom for an hour of reviewing, he began to experience the desire to study abroad. This motivated him to work hard at his present school courses in order to go abroad to further study science and technology in Europe and America in the future.

4.2.2 In the baseball contest that boy was the first one to bat a home run

In the second year of junior high school, he had a P.E. teacher surnamed Lin, who was a good baseball coach and an umpire. Lin selected nine boys from each class to be one team, and two teams played against each other on Mondays, Wednesdays and Fridays after class.

After testing him for catching, the boy was designated as a 'short stop,' catching the short distance, high flying, strong ball or the low ball rolling quickly on the ground, and standing between the second and third bases or behind the pitcher.

The boy was not very good at basketball and volleyball, but he was the best batter on his baseball team. After months of practice, he was the first one on the team to hit a home run.

After having fetched so much water for the vegetables, as well as the precise technique of swinging the bat, he became a very strong player. He hit the ball at a 45-degree parabola, and it flew from one end of the athletic field to the other end, coming down into a nearby paddy field.

He put the bat on the ground beside the home plate, ran to the first, second, and third bases, and finally back to home base. The defensive center outfielder was still looking for the ball in the paddy field, because the rice paddies grew to two feet tall, and it was difficult to find the ball in the water.

His team members screamed, applauded and jumped up and down. His coach, Lin, was especially happy. He laughed so much that he could not keep his mouth shut, for he felt that he was teaching pretty well.

The baseball team was dissolved after only one year. The umpire was hit by the ball, and he hadn't been wearing a chest protector. The pitcher threw the ball, but the catcher didn't catch it. It hit an important portion of the umpire, who jumped up and down for about three minutes. The game was continued, and he went back to being an umpire.

At that time, the school had no budget to buy those baseball accessories. It can be imagined how poor the school was then. If the team had continued to play for two more years, it might have become a good team. But he lost the chance to be trained as a good baseball player.

4.2.3 Being selected as an academic section chief

After getting a good score one semester, the boy was chosen as the academic section chief. After the academic section chief had collected enough writings from his classmates, he drew a picture of an irrigation machine with wooden wheels. Under the picture was depicted its function explained in English.

At that time, no one had seen a Chinese bulletin with English illustrations. About 10 classmates submitted more than 10 articles and pictures, which were pasted on a large piece of cardboard and posted on the wall behind the classroom, so that every student could read it. The teacher required every class to make a big wall bulletin every semester.

4.2.4 Selected to attend the Mandarin Speech Contest

He was also designated by a Mandarin teacher to attend a speech contest. The qualifications for contestants were: Mandarin pronunciation should be standard and correct, and the capability of composition must be very high, because the speech had to be written in advance and memorized.

The speech contest was performed in the auditorium, where the contestants would meet hundreds of people face to face. After he had finished writing his speech, he recited it again and again at home, until every word in the speech would never be forgotten.

But he didn't get any awards for the speech, because it was not good enough to get third place. Thankfully, though, he spoke in such a fluent way that he did not have to take out the speech draft to look at it.

4.3 The third year in junior high school

4.3.1 Designated a class monitor of the final semester

The second semester of third year junior high school, the first day of school, the classroom teacher Yu Ji Ue announced that the boy would be the class monitor because he'd had the highest scores for the previous semester.

The class monitor's duty was to coordinate and convey the problems between the teacher and the students. The most important job was whenever the teacher step into the classroom door, the class monitor would shout: "Stand up! Salute! Sit down!" Then the students stood up immediately from their chairs and bowed before they sat down. It was also the responsibility of the class monitor to supervise the academic, recreational, disciplinary and health: four section chiefs in four departments.

After the flag-raising ceremony, if the principal had some important news, the woman employee rang the bell hanging in the corridor in front of the principal's office. The monitors would then come to the bell, listen to the principal's important news, and then go back to their class to report the news to the other students.

Being a class monitor was his glory and pride after two years of studying diligently. Many students tried unsuccessfully to accomplish this goal.

4.3.2 The adoptive father promised that the boy could continue his studies

As the exam day neared, his classmate Chen asked the boy whether they could study together at his house to review for the entrance examination. Since the adopted boy was the class monitor, he could ask for help with the questions he didn't know.

They spent more than two weeks studying together after classes. One night, they studied until after 12 o'clock, and Chen decided to spend the night in the boy's home so they could study even longer.

The next morning his classmate Chen saw his adoptive father and asked him, "Uncle! uncle! If he wants to continue his studies, do you allow him to continue to study?"

"As long as he has the capability to study, I would let him go to as many schools as he wants," answered the adoptive father with a serious attitude.

4.3.3 Coping with any contingency on his graduation trip

The junior high school graduates had three classes of about 80 students, but only about 40 students joined the graduation trip. The boy was lucky enough to participate in the trip.

On the morning of their departure, his classmate Chen promised to come to his home first, and then the two of them could go together to the railway station. But when they arrived at the station, the train had just left a moment before, and they decided to take the next train.

The boy was still so young that he never took the train alone. This showed he could cope with the contingency to make the decision so quick that they caught up next train to complete the trip, instead of giving it up.

The boy checked the travel itinerary that the teacher had given him. The first stop was Hsinchu, about 30 minutes south of Taoyuan. So the two of them used their own money to buy two tickets, waited for one hour, and took the next train to Hsinchu.

At that time, 68 years ago, there were no taxis, only tricycles. After they got off the train, they hired a tricycle to go to the Hsinchu Grand Hotel.

Only the successful completion of this interesting episode was still remembered by him years later. The subsequent journey was completely forgotten.

4.3.4 Borrowing the 50 dollar registration fee from a neighbor for an entrance examination

In the summer of 1950, the registration date for the entrance examination was approaching. The boy had been deciding between entering the three-year high school or the five-year Taipei Institute of Technology (TIT). During that time, there was a five-year program at TIT that admitted junior high school graduates.

In other words, the educational system combined the three-year high school and four-year engineering college to become a five-year special institute of technology. If you were to graduate from the ordinary high school and the ordinary engineering college, the total school time required would be two more years than the special school. If you were entered in TIT, not only could you easily find a job after graduation, but also the education time was shorter and the cost was cheaper.

So he decided to take the five-year TIT (now the National Taipei University of Science and Technology (NTUST)). It took less time and less money, which suited his family's economic situation.

At that time, the registration fee for the Taipei Institute of Technology was NT $50, whereas the fee for the ordinary high school only $30. When the boy asked his adoptive mother for the registration fee, she said,

"I don't have that kind of money, and your father is now working in the south. Our family's economic condition means you can't continue to go to school." Then she walked away.

"This is my last chance to take the entrance examination of college," he pleaded, following her. "If I fail the exam, I won't take the ordinary high school exam. I will also do no more studies. I will concentrate on the learning of cement work to be a cement master in future, and will make money to support our family."

"Good! I will borrow 50 dollar from the next door aunt Chian tomorrow, so that you can register first. I will give it back to her when your father comes home, after he finishes the work in Jiayi." His mother turned around and left.

If he had not been admitted to the TIT at that time, he would never have had the chance to study again. At that time, the adoptive father's income was small and unstable. The adoptive mother often said that he worked far away from home, always sent money back late, the bottom of the rice crock was often seen, and she always borrowed rice from next door to support living.

The boy brought his 50 dollar fee, taking the train alone about half an hour to Taipei. After arriving at the station, he asked for directions to TIT, and then walked for 30 minutes to enroll at the registration office.

Even on the day of the exam, he took his lunch box alone to the examination. Whether he was in the examination room, on a break or at lunch, he was lonely. Not many 15-year-old boys handled their entrance exam processes all by themselves then.

4.3.5 Finally admitted to the
Taipei Institute of Technology

About a month after the exam, the school announced the admitted examinees for each department. The boy went to Taipei to see the exam bulletin. In the mechanical engineering examinees, he was listed in the seventh place.

He stared at his name for a few seconds, looked carefully again, and confirmed that it was his name. He began smiling, called his own name out, and then said, "I was admitted." The persons who were also looking at the bulletin stared at him, making him feel embarrassed as he walked away.

A class should have 30 students, but only about 15 examinees were listed. It was no wonder that there was a second examination to make up the number of students.

When he went home to tell the good news to his family, everyone was happy for him. Even the neighbors congratulated him. That moment was the most exciting, proudest moment of his life, and also the turning point of life.

This exam was the decision point of becoming a white collar worker or a blue collar worker, an engineer or a cement master. If he had not been admitted to the school this time, he would never have had another opportunity to walk through the gates of the school and get an education.

4.3.6 Summoned by the wife of the drawing teacher

There was a teacher who taught drawing in the same school. He had a son also graduating that year, but not in the same class.

After the graduation ceremony, the teacher's wife asked her son to invite the boy to her home to get acquainted with her, because she appreciated that he was the first native student of their home town to be admitted to the Taipei Institute of Technology that year.

Due to the rain, that year's graduation ceremony was held in the auditorium. When the ceremony finished and he was about to leave, her son hurried to stop him.

"My mother said she wanted to see you," said her son.

"Why does your mother want to see me?" the boy asked, surprised.

"I don't know, but you'll know when you see her," her son said.

The boy didn't ask him any more questions and followed him to his house.

The teacher lived in the Japanese-style teacher dormitories provided by the school on the other side of the athletic field. Since it had rained two days before, the athletic field was not completely dry, so as the boy walked on the wet track field, the mud and grass stuck to his shoes. (At that time, there was still no cement on the ground.)

When the boy got to the teacher's front porch, she had been waiting for a while.

"Please come in!" she said.

"I walked across the athletic field and there is mud and grass on my shoes, so I don't want to go in," the boy said politely.

"Never mind! You can take off your shoes and come up inside," she said.

"No! no! Thank you for inviting me to your house. What do you want to know? We can talk on the front porch," he answered.

Actually, he had never been in a Japanese-style house and felt embarrassed about going in. She wanted to know exactly how he had been studying to become a class monitor in the final semester, and was admitted to Taipei Institute of Technology (TIT).

In the other two classes of the same school year, the class monitors had not been changed within three years, and no one had ever been admitted to that school. She thought that his way of studying must be different from the others, and this was one of the reasons she had summoned him. The other reason was that she knew he was from a poor family.

Later she asked him something about his ordinary daily life, and also learned that his free time, when other students entertained themselves, was spent helping his family.

She was so pleased with the boy's success that she eventually urged her second son to be admitted to the top medical school in Taiwan, and her older son followed in his father's footsteps to become a drawing teacher.

5 Five years of Taipei Institute of Technology(TIT)

5.1 First year of TIT

Classmates taking the picture in front of school gate Taiwan Provincial Taipei Institute of Technology(TIT) (1950 to 1955)

5.1.1 Some anecdotes in the classroom

Before his class, Chen, the Mandarin teacher, used to talk to the students about the recent news, or some ancient poetry, the most interesting of which is the Limerick:

"One fate, two lucky, three chances, four moralities, five studies"

He said that study was listed last, implying that the first four items were more important than it. Without the first four items, only depending on study, one's achievements would be limited.

That boy also added to what the teacher said:

"The destiny of a person is already decided, and the result of struggle in one's life is limited."

There was a sports teacher surnamed Wu, who held a 100-meter race. Three students ran around 12 seconds, and that boy was one of them.

On rainy days, P.E. class was held in the classroom. The teacher Wu usually wore a short-sleeved white sports shirts and a casual suit outside. When he was talking about how to save money, he suddenly took off his casual suit, turned his back to the class, and let everyone see that his shirt had a ten-inch hole in the back.

The teacher explained that people should be frugal, and though the shirt was torn, it still could be worn.

This also showed, at that time, that the teachers' salary was very low, and when they had children, it really wasn't enough to support them.

5.1.2 Being a cement worker during the summer vacation

The school stipulated that every student should wear a work uniform during the factory practice. The shirt and the trousers were sewn together; it looked like a house-painter's uniform.

When his adoptive mother knew that he needed a work uniform, she immediately took him to the tailor to have one made in light blue. This uniform was worn for the school factory practice, the watering of vegetables and being a cement worker.

In summer of 1950, his first year at the Taipei Institute of Technology, a three-story building was to be built next to the Datong Theater in the center of Taoyuan city. His adoptive father got the cement and red brick project from the owner, surnamed Wang. The building was located about a 10-minute walk from home.

The boy, wearing the school work uniform, worked with two of his adoptive father's apprentices for the whole summer vacation. As a handyman, he did preparatory work, helped the two apprentices carry water, sand, pebble, brick and cement, and mix the cement with pebbles for the cement master to lay and paste the brick walls and the concrete floors.

At that time, there was no cement mixer. The whole building was built piece by piece of brick and the workers carried the mixed concrete from the first floor to the third floor, but the column was made with reinforced steel bars and concrete.

The hardest job was to carry about 60 bricks to third floor from the ground floor. The boy carried the same number of bricks upstairs as the two apprentices were doing.

5.2 The second year of TIT

5.2.1 Joining the school choir

Choir practice was held after lunch; three classmates, Hong, Huang, and the boy all participated. After all the students reported, the conductor tested the sound range of each participant one by one: tenor, baritone, and bass. The boy and Hong sang tenor, while Huang sang bass.

The choir conductor was a famous singer and conductor, Zhu Yong- Cheng. He was invited every year for a New Year flag-raising ceremony in front of the presidential palace to conduct the singing of national anthem. The following year, unfortunately he died in a fire in Singapore.

The music evening festival of
Taipei Institute of Technology Choir (1952)

5.2.2 Acquiring a work-study scholarship

In winter, the school had a service of steaming students' bento. He went with his classmate to pick up the steamed bento, but he did not dare to eat in the classroom together, because his lunch box contained only cabbage and dry radish. He was afraid of being embarrassed in front of his classmates.

When his school uniform was wrinkled, his grandmother washed it, dipped it in rice slurry to stiffen it, and dried it under the sun. Her treatment made it look as if it had been ironed by a laundryman.

There was a work-study program for students from poor families. The first academic year, he got pretty good scores, hence, in his second year in the mechanical engineering department, he acquired a work-study scholarship, got NT80 yuan a month, and worked in his own department office. He wrote the syllabus by using a pen writing the wax paper on a steel plate after class, and he worked two times a week for an hour each time. Although the wage was very low, it did help with some monthly expenses.

5.2.3 Napping in calculus class

He had class six days a week, every day except Sunday. After coming home from school every day, before reviewing his lessons, he had to water the vegetables and carry the drinking water from the well for cooking. When his adoptive father's friends came, they would talk all night, disturbing the boy's studies, because the living room was also the study room.

Sometimes when his father's friend came over, he had to endure the talking and continue to do his homework there, because the next day there was an exam. In these situations he had to study until 1 or 2 o'clock and then get up at 5:30am to catch the 6:15am train to school.

In his second year, the calculus course was scheduled for the first period on Monday, Wednesday and Friday mornings. The boy went to school by train and then on foot, slept only six hours a day, and sometimes dozed off in calculus class.

He liked to sit in the front row of the classroom, and because he wore a pair of thick glasses, he thought the teacher could not see whether his eyes were open or closed. Though his body didn't move when he slept, eventually the teacher figured out that he was taking a nap and called his name, telling him not to doze off.

But after the mid-term exam, his test scores were so good that even though the teacher still caught him napping in the class, he didn't get in trouble for it.

Anyway, his test scores were good even with him napping in class, but if he hadn't napping due to not enough sleeping, the scores would have been much better.

5.2.4 Looking up a new word from a dictionary in English exams

Wu Kwang, a graduate of the famous Tsinghua University in China, was the English professor in the boy's class. Once in the English exam, the boy put a small book on his desk. Wu immediately walked to his desk, picked up the small book and opened it. Seeing that it was an English-English dictionary, he put it back on the desk and then walked away.

After a while, in the back of class room, his classmate Li also took out an English-Chinese dictionary and put it on his desk. The teacher went over and told him to put it back in his desk. Li pointed out that the boy had a dictionary, and asked why he could not use one. The teacher answered, "That boy is that boy, and you are you."

The teacher did not tell him the reason, and he was puzzled. After the exam, he asked the boy, and eventually he understood that the boy had used an English-English dictionary.

5.2.5 Taking part in the school English speech contest

When the school held an English speech contest, from each department, one contestant would be sent to attend the contest. At that time, the Taipei Institute of Technology had six engineering departments: mechanical, electrical, chemical, civil, mining and metallurgy, and architectural. They also had five-year and three-year programs.

Other departments selected a third-year student to attend, but the mechanical department chose a second-year student. Why did the English teacher designate him to represent the mechanical department?

He only remembered that the teacher asked him to stand up and read a paragraph of text, and decided to ask him to attend. Within two weeks, he wrote an article, and then memorized it.

On the day of the speech, the auditorium was crowded with hundreds of listeners. The speakers sat in the front row, and the boy was the fourth in line to go up to stage. From beginning to end, he never looked at the speech draft, and finished the whole speech fluently.

As the result, the boy had the shortest time. The other contestants had longer times, since all of them had stopped to look at their speeches once or twice. But he still did not get into within third place.

Later he analyzed why he had not done better. He had written the speech by himself and showed it to the English teacher, but the teacher did not make any changes to his speech or give him any suggestions. He decided the speech should have been more esoteric and longer.

5.2.6 Taipei City public bus repair shop internship

The school required that before graduation, each student would practice outside the factory for one month every summer vacation. That year, the boy applied to the Taipei City public bus repair shop for an internship.

The most intriguing thing to him was the overhaul of the car engine and the grinding of the cylinder inlet and outlet valves. In addition, Taipei City public buses treated the intern very well. During the internship he was free to take the Taipei City buses, so in his lunch time, he visited the scenery site of Green Lake.

At a 30-minute bus ride to the outskirts of the country, there was a rather famous town named Scenery Beautiful. Not only was the landscape beautiful, but there were mountains, water, bridges, and beneath the bridge, there was an unusual Green Lake.

5.3 Third year of the Taipei Institute of Technology (TIT)

5.3.1 Refusing the election to be a class monitor

The first day of the first semester in the third school year of TIT, because the current class monitor Hong quit the class monitor position for various reasons, the class needed to choose a new one.

The class monitor Hong immediately raised his hands to recommend that boy as a candidate of new class monitor to be voted on by their classmates. Before the election the boy stood up, saying that he did not have enough time to do this job. After school he had to help out at home, so he wouldn't have sufficient energy and time to deal with the class administration, and he tactfully refused the class monitor job.

At last, his classmate Chang, who lived in the school dormitory, became the class monitor. The boy was very envious of him being able to live in the schoolhouse, and of those students who lived in Taipei having more time to rest and study every day.

5.3.2 Napping in a standing position when the train was moving

Because sometimes that boy studied until after 12 o'clock at night, the next day he would nap standing up while the train was moving. If he couldn't find a seat, so he learned to sleep standing up. Leaning against the back of a chair, and clutching it with both hands, his body would sway with the train's motion. At first he was not accustomed to sleeping in this position.

After a year of taking the train to school, he developed the ability to stand and nap: as long as his feet were a little bit apart and his hands firmly grasped the backrest of the seat, usually he could nap to the next stop, when the train stopped to let passengers off. This was the way that he made up his lack of sleep.

5.3.3 Factory practice in the Railway Repair Depot of Taiwan Railway Administration

The third year of summer break, the adopted boy chose the Taiwan Railway Repair Depot in Pine Hill district, Taipei, as his second factory internship. He practiced in the Railway Bureau, and every day his ticket to the repair shop back and forth was free, as it had been in Taipei the year before.

Most students chose a factory where they could work after graduation, but he selected the factory related to transportation such as automobiles, trains, ships, or airplanes.

For the first time, he saw the internal structure of the locomotive with so many dense steam tubes, though he was seeing the outside appearance of the locomotive every day. This plant not only repaired steam locomotives, but also repaired diesel-powered diesel vehicles. Trains were driven by the steam power of burning coal to drive steel wheels on two tracks, while the ordinary diesel cars were powered by the diesel explosion power to drive rubber tires running on ordinary roads. But the railroad's diesel-car's wheels, like the wheels of the train, were steel wheels, and ran on two rails.

There were no electrical or magnetic trains 65 years ago. Maybe in another 65 years, people will sit inside a small rocket cabin to fly around in the sky as everyday vehicles!

After the diesel engine was repaired, he asked the repair technician whether he could sit in the diesel car which was ready to test run, and the mechanic agreed. The test of diesel vehicles was only between two train stations: from Taipei to Pan Chiao.

Usually the diesel cars were packed with passengers, but today, the car was so empty that no passenger was riding it except the driving test technician and the boy. He was sitting alone in the two-box diesel car, feeling very excited, and this was the only chance he'd had for such enjoyment in his life.

As soon as the diesel car was tested very stable and not shaking, it was driven back to the repair factory.

5.4 Fourth year of TIT

5.4.1 Factory Internship in Taiwan shipyard

In 1953, that boy applied to the Taiwan shipyard as his third off-campus factory internship.

The shipyard was located in a place called "Peace Island," which was situated at the north of Keelung, north of Taipei. There was a bridge spanning north Keelung and Peace Island.

The location of the factory internship was too far from Taoyuan, so the adoptive mother arranged for him to live with a sworn sister in Keelung. But his aunt's economic situation was not very good, so the adoptive mother gave his aunt his expense monthly for rooming and board.

Every day after breakfast, his aunt always gave him a bento box, then he took the city bus to the Peace Island Factory. It was the first time he had seen a merchant ship parked inside a dry dock, and from outside the dock he could see the blue glow on the hull surface, which was caused by the workers welding.

When a merchant ship or oil tanker was to be repaired, the ship entered the dock, the water inside the dock was pumped out to become a dry dock, and then the repairmen started to repair the faulty part.

The director of the dock and the repair shop was Mr. Wu, who was from his same hometown and also from his school.

It was a pity that the factory wouldn't let the intern aboard the ship to see the detailed structure and the actual repair situation.

5.4.2 In day time practicing in the shipyard; at night time attending English typing class

During the shipyard internship, at nighttime, walking through Keelung Harbor and city streets, that boy happened to see an advertisement posted on the windows for typing classes.

So he enrolled in the class: one hour per lesson, three nights a week of classes, a one-month typing class, with a certificate of completion at the end of the study.

English typing was not very common at that time. If the speed of typing per minute exceeded a certain standard, a job could be found in the foreign trade company.

But he thought that the use of typewriters would be popular in the future, and the typewriter could be owned individuals. Sure enough, eventually typewriters began to be used in every company and even owned privately.

5.4.3 Being a cement worker for the second time

In the summer vacation of 1954, the adoptive father contracted the construction of cement works in six new houses opposite to the rear door of East Gate Elementary School.

This was the second time that boy worked as a cement worker for two months. His skill was so good that he could have been hired by an outside constructor to do the cement work.

But this was not what his adoptive father wanted. He wanted him to study seriously, so he could improve his condition.

5.4.4 Visiting one classmate, Hung, during an internship in Keelung shipyard

On the way to the Keelung shipyard for his internship, the boy visited his classmate Hong, who lived in Pah Tuu. When he arrived at Hung's house at the agreed time, Hung and his mother were already waiting at the door.

Hung's mother looked gentle and kind. The two classmates chatted for a while, and as the boy began to leave, Hung said that his mother had already cooked lunch. The boy was embarrassed to refuse, and finally had to take lunch together with them. To have eaten lunch 60 years ago, now the adopted boy says thanks again to them!

5.5 Fifth year of TIT

5.5.1 Using a typewriter to type instead of a steel plate to write for the work-study program

On the first day of the fifth school year, the boy went to the mechanical engineering office and told the director that he had learned how to type in English. Because it was not very popular to use a typewriter at the time, there was no typewriter or typist employed in this office.

After finding that the boy was capable of English typing, the department chief immediately asked his assistant to buy a typewriter. Since then, the mechanical engineering department began to have an English typing machine, and the work-study program of that boy was also changed from writing with a steel plate to typing with a typewriter.

5.5.2 A field trip to the Shimen dam

In the spring of 1954, the boy took part in a trip sponsored by his class. The most memorable part was Shimen dam, a scenic spot. The dam was located about one hour from Taoyuan.

When the reservoir was just starting to be constructed, most of the forest, mountain, and streams still retained their original natural beauty, but only a small lake was kept beside the dam's machine room, and there were several people swimming in the lake.

After walking around the forest trail for about 30 minutes, all of the classmates went back to the nearby hotel for a rest.

5.5.3 During these five years without fail the grandma cooked breakfast at five o'clock in the morning

During those five years, if his grandmother had not gotten up early and cooked breakfast at five o'clock every weekday, there would have been no way for the boy to attend his first lesson. Then he wouldn't have obtained good grades, and wouldn't have been able to graduate from that school.

After having been overworked for a very long time, his grandmother suffered from high blood pressure, and had her first stroke when he was working in Taiwan. She eventually died from her third stroke, when the boy was still studying in the U.S.A.

Because his adoptive mother often helped his adoptive father working outside, the cooking and laundry were done by the grandmother.

His grandmother was a typical Taiwanese lady with kindness, endurance, patience, and devotion.

In her whole life, she had been working uncomplainingly and selflessly for the family, and never asked for rewards. Her love for her grandson was the greatest, most incomparable love in the world. That boy has always remembered and been grateful for his grandmother's love!

6 Working in the brick kiln factory after graduating from TIT

Waiting for the army training, the boy worked in the brick kiln factory

for three months. The kiln had three partners: a carpenter and two cement master workers. His adoptive father was one of the partners. Each partner took turns at being the director, and stayed in the factory to operate the kiln.

The factory site was located in the outskirts of Taoyuan, about 30 minutes away from Taoyuan, in a village named Pa De. The boy went to work by bus from Taoyuan to the factory every day. The brick kiln factory was mainly composed of two sections: two brick-cutting machines and two brick-burning kilns.

The job of the boy was to supervise the workers who cut the red mud and pushed it into the kilns. It was not easy to burn good bricks. It was a pity that he couldn't see the process of lighting the fires inside the kiln, because it was always done after he went home. When he went to work the next day, he saw smoke curling up from the top of the chimney to the azure sky.

Because a good brick master couldn't be found, the factory was sold after several years, when the boy was in America.

7 Military training of the Reserved Officer Training Corp (ROTC)

At that time, according to government regulations, all male college graduates were required to complete a one-year military training in ROTC. For the first month, all college graduates were trained at Feng Shan Military Officer Academy for their basic training, and then based on their department in college, they were distributed to the different military camps.

After one month of basic training, he was assigned to the air force base at Taichung, located in the middle part of Taiwan, for his practical training. The most exciting course in the basic training program was shooting. Three days before the end of the one-month training, he used a carbine gun to shoot 50 rounds of live ammunition. Since he was interested in shooting, later coming to America, he sometimes went to the "Target Master" store to shoot.

He practiced in the Quality Management Department of the C-46 and C-47 aircraft repair plant. Every day he sat in front of the desk, filled up the repair schedule to post on the wall, and the aircraft was repaired following the schedule. Hence, he got a chance to get near the aircraft, and was able to see every part of the aircraft thoroughly and clearly.

Compared to practicing at school, the city bus repair shop, the train repair shop, and the shipyard, the aircraft repairing practice had a much better chance to look in detail, and longer time to study.

One Sunday, he took C–47 propeller-type cargo plane with three other trainees from the Clear Water Air Force Airport to the Taipei Pine Hill Airport, and then took the train from Taipei back to Taoyuan. It was his first time flying back to Taoyuan in his training period; it was also his first time taking an airplane in his life.

8 Employed by the companies or factories in Taiwan

8.1 San Shang Machine Works

8.1.1 Getting a job without an employment exam by reading the newspaper's help wanted ads.

Time flies. In the blink of an eye, his year of military training was ended. The food at the training base was not bad, but in the cafeteria next door, the flight pilots' meals were much better. After lunch, the boy was reading newspapers and saw an advertisement for a mechanical designer at a factory in Taipei.

He thought that this was the kind of factory where he was going to work in future. When he came home for the holiday, he went to the stationery store, bought a blank resume, filled out the form, and mailed it immediately to the factory.

He wanted to work in a small factory like this, so that after he got some experience and some capital, he could set up his own factory. He received an acceptance letter of employment before he was discharged from the military.

At that time, during the ten-year construction period for the whole county, the government held employment examinations for engineering graduates. But if the graduate had poor exam scores they were rejected for employment.

When he was still in the military service, he found a job, so he was not required to take the employment exam.

8.1.2 The first three-dimensional drawing in the factory

This factory, named "San Shang Machine Works," located on Fushun Street in Taipei City, was the province's oldest and most famous manufacturer. They made all kinds of pumps and blowers, and the boss, surnamed Xiao, had graduated from the same school as the boy did, but at a different time, during the Japanese era.

During his first year of work, he made a 3-D drawing of a one-meter-high plunger pump. A real plunger pump was drawn in a half scale on the blue drawing, which was hung on the wall, and let customers know that this factory could also draw a 3D size of the wall chart.

The plunger pump was later taken to the exhibition sponsored by the Taiwan Machinery Industry Association.

Apparently, before he entered the factory, the boss had asked the previous school factory practice director Chen, to check on his school records. After he had worked in this factory for several months, the director Chen visited this factory. Before the director was leaving, his boss and he both said the appreciations to the director.

The boy hosted the San Shang Machine works exhibition (1957)
Sponsored by Taiwan Machinery Industry Association

8.1.3 Losing the chance to set up a factory

After working at the machine factory for three years, the foreman, Shaw, wanted to quit his job, and proposed to the boy to set up a factory with him.

At that time, the 23-year-old adopted boy was also trying to set up a factory. To do so required 30,000 NT dollars. But the families of the adopted boy couldn't raise the funds, and the opportunity to set up a factory in the partnership was lost. It was the first great setback of his life.

If the family could have raised the funds or borrowed the money, he would have set up a factory, and then he wouldn't have gone to study abroad.

When he first returned to Taiwan to visit his family, the boy was told that the previous foreman Shaw, who was a partner of a factory, had opened a pump factory on the outskirts of Taipei. He also went to visit the new boss Shaw, but he happened to be out on the job site supervising installation work.

8.2 Tien Li Motor Company

8.2.1 Director of the pump development department

He decided to switch to another factory to work when he couldn't set up a factory by himself. At the same time, the Tien Li Motor Company had just published a recruitment ad for a pump designer in the newspaper. The boy sent in his resume to apply, and as a result he was hired as the pump development department director.

The factory had previously cooperated with the Japanese factory technologically, so the motors and electric fans were excellent and famous. The purpose of his being hired was to connect both pumps and motors together, so that the two machines could be sold at the same time.

Within a year, he developed a variety of pumps that the boss had asked for, and beside the building built a triangular water trough made by the concrete and the brick to test the pump flow rate.

8.2.2 Quit office for not keeping a promise to raise the salary

After a year of work at this company, the boss didn't give him the pay raise he had promised, so the boy began to read the help wanted section of the newspaper.

A Chinese oil company advertised for engineers. He mailed his resume to apply and after about a week, an acceptance letter was sent to his home.

After receiving the hiring letter, he immediately tendered his resignation to the company and reported to the oil company.

8.3 Engineering Department of Business Section of China Petroleum Company

8.3.1 Supervising the welding project of the floating roof petroleum tank

After a period of training at the Taipei Head Office's engineering department, all new engineers were sent to visit the Jiayi oil exploration section office and the Kaohsiung Refinery.

Then the boy was assigned to Pa Tu Oil Depot. The company provided a dormitory for room and board at Taipei, but the employees had to pay for it. Every day he took the company car to the oil depot to work.

When the construction of a floating roof oil tank for storing fuel was just starting to be built, he was appointed to oversee the welding work.

8.3.2 Marine gas station "the captain of the flagship"

After the project of the floating roof oil tank was completed, the boy was transferred to the marine gas station at Keelung Reservoir as a station head: besides eight crew members, there were an oil barge and a tugboat.

They dubbed the tugboat the flagship and the boy the captain.

For fishing boats, the diesel oil was filled up directly at the gas station; however, when fueling international merchant ships, he sat in the tugboat's driving cabin as the tugboat was driven by a real captain. They hauled the barge, fully loaded with diesel oil, to the sea off the coast of Keelung harbor, where the ship waited for fueling.

On one occasion, when a foreign tanker was fueling from a barge, he climbed up to the deck of a large tanker to visit the piping's wiring arrangement.

8.3.3 Obtaining a full scholarship for studying in American university

During the training in the Taipei head office of the petroleum company, nine out of ten trainees were the alumni of the Taipei Institute of Technology (TIT), but only one colleague, Li, had graduated from the mechanical engineering department of Taiwan University (TU), and pretty soon he was going to study in the United States.

Li also said that ninety percent of students in his class were ready to study abroad. The boy wondered why only TU students could study abroad. It was as if studying abroad was their invention. If TU students could, then of course TIT students should also be able to.

Because of having attended the "internal combustion engine" class taught by Professor Jin Zu Neang at both TU and TIT, the boy became excited at the idea of continuing his studies.

"Can you tell me how to apply for an American school?" he asked his colleague Li.

"All you have to do is go to the Taipei Library, look for the American University Profile Handbook section on the bookshelf, pull out the school catalog you want to apply to, and the catalog will explain how to apply to the school," Li answered simply and straightforwardly.

From his colleague's advice, the door to study abroad had been opened for the boy. This was another turning point in his life, so Li could be seen as one of his life mentors.

The next day, he borrowed three American university catalogs from the library, then went to TIT to apply for three copies of the school records, and sent three copies of the school records, three copies of school enrollment and two copies of scholarship applications to three different schools.

As a result, the University of South Dakota sent a full scholarship letter and the academy entrance certificate, while the University of California at Los Angeles only sent a tuition-free letter and the graduate school entrance certificate.

8.3.4 Proof of exemption from the exam to study abroad

At that time, all the students who wanted to go abroad to study had to take a studying abroad examination conducted by the Ministry of Education. But the Ministry of Education had just added a new provision: students who obtained a full scholarship and a graduate school admission letter could be exempted from the examination.

The boy immediately sent his full scholarship notice and admission letters to the Ministry of Education, but after about a month, he had still obtained no exemption letter from the education department. He went to the Office of Ministry of Education to inquire. It was the first year that the exemption policy had been introduced, and there were a lot of students who had applied for it, so the time to process the applications took a little longer than usual. However, after another three days, the letter of exemption was sent to his home.

8.3.5 Smoothly obtaining a visa from the U.S. consulate

When he went to the U.S. consulate, he took the University of California's tuition-free letter and entrance certificate for the visa. The consul said that he was also graduated from the University of California, Los Angeles, and that he should take the English class in the U.S.A, so not only did he have no written exam, but also no oral exam, and he immediately obtained his visa.

At that time, the United States Embassy was still stationed in Taiwan. Only graduate students could go abroad for advance study, and it was not an easy thing to do.

Nowadays, studying abroad does not require an exam, and it is not limited. Anybody who wants to can go abroad to study or travel.

9 Departing the home country

On September 1, 1962, the boy was to leave his home country to go abroad to study. All of his family members and relatives sat in front of their house and took a photo as a memory.

More than 50 years ago in Taiwan, the airplane flying to the foreign country was from the Taipei Song San Airport; the airplane was a Japanese airlines jet aircraft. It was parked at a distance away from the building, so the boy had a long walk to reach it, and then climbed the steps to enter the airplane.

When he arrived at the airport, all his family members and friends came to say farewell to him. But he especially wants to thank his classmate Wang again for taking his group pictures.

From the customs building, he had to walk outdoors for about two or three minutes, then went up the stairs to the plane, and turned to face the crowd. They were so far away that he could not see who was who, but he waved and then went into the cabin.

10 The first day stepping on American territory

10.1 The colleague Li picked up that boy from the airport

A week before he left Taiwan, he had written to the Lansun Li colleagues to tell them when he would arrive in Los Angeles. Therefore, as soon as he got out of customs, his colleague Li was waiting at the exit gate.

Li drove him to his rented house near UCLA, where two other students were already living temporarily. Everything had been arranged by his colleague.

11 University of California at Los Angeles (UCLA)

11.1 The first quarter at UCLA

11.1.1 US President was assassinated

At UCLA, the school year was divided into four quarters, which was different from the three semesters systems it was used to be. At the beginning of October, the UCLA school year began. Li had also rented a two-bedroom house for four students: a younger brother and an elder sister lived in one room, while a student named Wang and the boy lived in another room.

The rental house was located on the other side of the school athletic field, and every weekday it took more than 15 minutes to cross the field to get to his classes.

After he had been attending classes for about one month, he was walking home one day through the athletic field, when he suddenly saw several girls crying there. The United States national anthem was also playing, and then the news that the United States President John F Kennedy had been assassinated was announced.

11.1.2 First part-time job in America

Having taken classes for a week, that boy went to a nearby Italian restaurant to eat dinner. The waiter gave him a menu and he read it through from the first page to the last page, finding that the cheapest food was a piece of pizza for a dollar. It was 12 inches in diameter. After he had eaten half of the pizza, the waiter walked up to him.

"I'm looking for a job, do you have anything I could do?" the boy asked him.

"Wait a minute, let me ask the boss. Mario..." the waiter answered, yelling the boss's name as he went into the kitchen.

"What kind of work can you do?" the boss came out and asked him.

"I can do anything but be a chef," said he, daring to answer.

"Okay, you come five o'clock in the afternoon tomorrow. Wear a white shirt and black tuxedo trousers." The boss gave him a job on the spot.

On the next day at five o'clock in the afternoon, he arrived on time to report to the boss Mario. His job was to prepare salad materials as a salad man. First he cleaned the green salad, cut it into small pieces, made a salad bowl, and cut salami and ham to make a cold plate-antipasto. Nowadays, every time he eats a slice of pizza, he thinks of his first part-time job in America. At that time a piece of pizza cost a dollar, but the current price is about 20 times that.

With his agreement to the creditor, when he found a job and received his first paycheck, he should return the borrowed money to the lender in full amounts. The next day he went to the bank to buy a bank's cashier check and sent it back to Taiwan by registered mail.

The Italian restaurant did not pay much; so during the day he also went to work for a company called the Payne Heater Company. He worked four hours a day; spent two hours in the bus back and forth traveling; therefore, he only worked for a couple months, and then quit that job.

11.1.3 Getting stabbed in the finger by a knife tip

The types of students who come to the United States to work in restaurants are: waiters, bus boys, runners, dishwashers, and those who prepare salads, called the salad man.

Only Italian restaurants had a salad man, and he did that job. After the customer ordered a plate of antipasto (Italian dish), the attendants went to the kitchen to order food for the customer.

To get a plate of antipasto, it needed to be ordered first. The boy often held a small meat knife in his right hand,

and one time a waiter approached him suddenly, waving his hands. The waiter's left hand hit his right hand, and the knife stabbed into his own left hand ring finger, immediately causing severe bleeding.

The boss hurriedly put a bandage on to stop the bleeding. Though his finger hurt for awhile, he continued working; and even now a scar of about 10 millimeters in diameter is still faintly visible. Hence, we can see that this boss cared enough about his employees to bandage them himself.

11.2 The second quarter in UCLA

11.2.1 Working in a restaurant near Hollywood Boulevard

After the previous quarter, from school he applied to a student dormitory to live with a political Korean student. The Korean student introduced him to a Hawaiian restaurant called Islanders, located on La Cinega Blvd, three blocks from Hollywood Boulevard.

But from school to this restaurant would take about 30 minutes by bus. From 7 to 11 o'clock at night, he was responsible for carrying large plates of cooked dishes to the customers; this kind of work is called the runner.

Once the restaurant business was so good that it was too late to catch the last bus, and he walked two hours to get back to his dorm. Fortunately, that night was bright moonlight, there were no pedestrians and only a few vehicles on the streets, and he felt lonely and silent. Another time, his class ended late; and in order to arrive at the restaurant on time, he had to hitchhike.

In the 1960s, hitchhiking was very common and safe, but now it's very dangerous.

One day, the boy saw a notice on the bulletin board outside the office of the engineering department, with an advertisement for a lab assistant.

The next day he went to the professor's lab early to apply. The professor said one sentence: "The early bird gets the worm," but did not say anything else, and asked him to work the next day. The hours were every Monday, Wednesday and Friday from one to two o'clock in the afternoon.

11.3 The third quarter at UCLA

11.3.1 Working at a farm during summer vacation

In the summer vacation, three civil engineering students from Taiwan University asked him to go with them to the Washington State Walla Walla farm to work for one month.

A total of four students rode in the car, starting 8 o'clock in the morning. The student named Chang drove northward to the farm. It was almost sunset when they arrived. After reporting to the office, they were assigned to live in temporary barracks. All of them were students coming from foreign countries and the domestic United States.

The next day, early in the morning, as soon as they finished breakfast, they were loaded into the big truck and taken to the green bean field. This kind of American round green bean was about three times bigger than the Chinese small green bean, and boiled to be a salty bean to eat, but was not boiled to be a sweet green bean soup.

Each person was assigned to the back of the automatic bean-cutting machine. The green bean was automatically dialed out and sent to the square slot at the back end of the car, and after the slot was full, it was quickly moved to the truck and driven away. So the truck carried load after load of green bean boxes away, and he worked straight through until sunset.

One month of work was not hard; but in the morning and evening, the biting wind and a whole day of the machine engine's manic sound was almost unbearable.

The latitudes of Los Angeles, California and Walla Walla, Washington were 10 degrees different, and that why the later location was much colder than the former.

12 University of Southern California (USC)

12.1 During the day, worked full-time at the construction company; at night worked part-time in the restaurant

After the boy came back from the farm, he went to UCLA to get a bachelor's degree certificate, and then applied to the graduate program at USC. Before the start of the autumn season, he continued to work in the Hawaiian restaurant near Hollywood, and was living in the vicinity of USC.

The USC had daytime and night courses, designed for people who were employed during the day. He chose to take night courses.

After the semester began, in the daytime he worked for the HVAC department of the K Engineering Co. in downtown Los Angeles, and in the evening he took courses for his master's degree.

12.2 The first semester of the first year of USC

12.2.1 Professor's assistant of mechanical engineering

In his first year at USC, he found a job as a teaching assistant, and quit his job at the engineering company. The teaching assistant's job was to correct the students' homework for the professor, and he wouldn't have to work if the students didn't have any homework.

He used the theory of solid, liquid and gas changes in thermodynamics to make a teaching model made by using the plastic boards and nylon threads.

12.2.2 Managing a 16-unit apartment complex

When looking for an apartment, he happened to find one for rent in the vicinity of USC. The current occupant was the manager of the apartments, an Iranian student who was returning to his hometown in the near future.

The manager of the 16-unit apartment complex told him that he would have to be the manager of the complex if he wanted to rent the unit.

He said he did not have any experience in management, but the manager said it was very easy. The manager's jobs were: collect the monthly rent from the existing tenants and get the application forms from the expecting tenants, and notify the landlord when the inside units needed repairing and the tenants wanted to move out. Then, the landlord would handle such things himself.

He agreed to take the job. The landlord was a first generation Japanese immigrant. Since the boy could also speak Japanese, their communication was very easy, so the landlord valued him very much. He not only rented an apartment, but also got a manager job.

12.3 The second semester of the first year in USC

12.3.1 His first son was born

It was the Taiwanese custom that when a baby is born, the mother eats sesame oil chicken to nourish her body. Moreover, the boy provided the glutinous fried rice for the other Taiwanese folks living in their apartment.

Since he became the manager of the apartments, students from Taiwan gradually began moving in. Eventually 94% of the residents came from Taiwan. Only one unit was occupied by an American family. Since the apartments looked like a Taiwanese village, everybody dubbed him "the chief" of the Taiwan village.

12.4 The first semester of the second year in USC

12.4.21 Recruited by the Boeing Aircraft Company

After the boy went to the mechanical engineering department office to discuss his course with a professor, he saw a bulletin board outside the office with a recruiting notice from Boeing.

He immediately prepared a resume and a copy of his transcript to apply to Boeing in the designated classroom. After waiting for two weeks, he received an offer of employment, and he jumped up and down with joy. After another semester, he got his master's degree in mechanical engineering and drove north to report to Boeing.

12.5 Second semester of the second year in USC

12.5.1 Declining Hewlett Packard's offer of employment

That boy had always thought that it would be excellent to work in a big company in Los Angeles. Then he saw an advertisement from Hewlett-Packard recruiting engineers in the Los Angeles Times. He sent his resume and the school transcript to that company. After two weeks, he received another job offer, but the starting salary per month was 15 percent less than Boeing offered.

At that time, for a foreign student, 15 percent of the salary could be used to pay one month's rent. HP was a small company then producing the X-Y printer. Nowadays HP is much larger, making electronic products as famous as IBM, Apple, and Dell.

In order to get a better income every month, he chose to work at Boeing. If he'd chosen HP, it might have been possible for him to set up his own factory, because to establish a small electronics-related factory required much less capital than an airplane company did.

13 Reporting to Boeing by driving north along the 101 Interstate

13.1 Overnight at Yosemite National Park

In his offer letter, Boeing provided a moving allowance: it would cover the expense of taking an airplane or driving a car, and the hotel cost for two weeks after reporting to the head office.

The boy chose to drive instead of flying, so his family could sightsee along the way. In July 1967, starting from Los Angeles in the morning at eight o'clock, they arrived at the south entrance of Yosemite National Park around noon.

Shortly after entering the park, he saw a hotel and immediately booked a room for a night. Next morning, after breakfast, he drove along the road, and saw two waterfalls: Yosemite Falls and Bridal Veil Falls, the world's tallest waterfalls. Besides that, they also saw Half Dome. The park was built in 1890 and designated by the nation as the third national park.

It was not only a great valley but also a shrine to human foresight, the power of glaciers, the persistence of life, and the tranquility of the High Sierra. Yosemite National Park, one of the first wilderness parks in the United States, was best known for its waterfalls, but within its nearly 1,200 square miles, you could find deep valleys, grand meadows, ancient sequoias – red wood, and a vast wilderness area.

13.2 Driving along Interstate 101 to Boeing for work

Highway 101 extends up the Pacific Ocean coast, through the states of California, Oregon, and Washington. The boy drove along this highway from Los Angeles, through San Francisco and up to Seattle. You can't get lost if you drive along Highway 101.

While driving, looking the ocean was an endless pleasure.

After all these years of work and study, study and work, he was exhausted. But his struggle was finally rewarded, and he had obtained a high-paying job.

After a whole day of seeing the vast ocean, all the mental pressure and physical tiredness disappeared completely, and he felt as light as a feather floating in the air. In particular, he enjoyed the seaside highway in the state of Oregon, seeing the sea lions swaying left and right, crawling on the rocks or taking a nap on the beach, and also hearing their singing.

Getting into Washington State, from a distance you could see the top of Mt. Rainier, which looked as if it wore a white hat. They arrived at the Boeing headquarters in Renton as the sun was nearly going into ocean. He quickly reported to the company's personnel office, and eventually a hotel was found nearby for his family to live in.

14 Working in Boeing and further studies

14.1 First year at Boeing

14.1.1 Boeing 757 new Aircraft Research and Development

Because the company paid only two weeks of hotel accommodation, on Sunday the boy began to look for a house near Washington University in Seattle for his family. Mr. Ting, a fellow-countryman in Los Angeles, introduced him to his younger brother, who was already working at Boeing.

After the boy moved to Seattle, he telephoned the brother to get acquainted. The boy was hired as a research engineer and assigned to the Boeing 757 Airplane Research and Development Department.

14.1.2 The boy and his supervisor smoke each other's pipes

There was still no smoking ban then, and even in the office, every worker could smoke at their desks. The boy was assigned to sit in front of his supervisor. On one occasion, when he had a question to ask his boss Bill Larson, he just directly rotated his chair 180 degrees to face his supervisor, and the two of them discussed the problems.

The two of them had put their pipes on the same desk, and suddenly the supervisor picked up one of the pipes to smoke, and that boy also pick up another pipe to smoke, but nobody knew which one belonged to whom. Then the supervisor saw that they were smoking each other's pipes, and they returned their pipes to each other, laughing.

The two pipes were almost of the same size and color, and were difficult to identify. The relationship between the two of them was so harmonious, and even now that boy still remembers and thinks about his supervisors.

14.1.3 Requesting two-month-long vacation to visit his hometown

According to the company regulations, every employee had two weeks' vacation every year. If an employee didn't take a vacation one year, he could take a month in next year. The boy asked for a one-month vacation without waiting for his second year, and the personnel office approved.

But his supervisor said that if the company could approve a one-month vacation without waiting for the second year, it could be also allowed for one-year employment to have two months' vacation; therefore, the boy bravely requested a two-month-long special vacation.

During the midsummer, the Taiwan weather was burning hot, and with unbearably high humidity, because the location of Taiwan is closer to the equator than Seattle does.

Taiwan was the hometown of both the boy and his wife. Though they had only left five years from there, they still couldn't accommodate the weather there.

So every day they stayed at home with their family; only going to the surrounding areas near their hometown. They were afraid to travel overnight, and the furthest place they went was to Taipei to see the "I Love the Weekend" live night show.

The music conductor of a large TV station named Lin had been in the same class as the boy at the Taipei Institute of Technology for five years. During their class reunion, Lin had invited him to watch the "I Love the Weekend" evening live show, so he brought more than ten of his relatives to Taipei to see the show.

Before the show began, Lin called him up backstage to introduce Phoenix-fly-fly singer to him. Lin specially asked the video director to sweep the camera over the group who had come with the boy. Politicians and entertainers were either reported on newspapers every day, or often on camera.

Engineering personnel usually didn't get to be in newspapers or on TV in their lifetime, even though they were engaged in the construction of structures that humans relied on for survival. So engineers were "unsung heroes."

14.2 The first year of the University of Washington

14.2.1 Starting to take PhD courses

Large American companies would often help employees pay for tuition, and Boeing was no exception when their employees applied to study.

The boy told his supervisor he wanted to work and study at the same time, and he submitted a master degree certificate, a school record, and an application form for the University of Washington (UW). A month later, the school sent a certificate of admission and the boy began his work–study career.

Shortly after he began his studies, he received a letter from the mechanical engineering department, formally accepting him as a candidate for the doctoral program. Moreover, four advisors were appointed, with Professor Brown as his principal advisor. The UW campus was so beautiful in the autumn with red–yellow leaves on the trees and the ground, and occasionally blowing up to the azure sky in the wind.

In 1962, for the World Fair, a Space Needle was built in the Seattle city center. It's a grand scenic spot!

14.2.2 Visiting places of interest near Seattle

This was the boy's first time in Seattle, and everything was new for his family. So every weekend or holiday, he always took his family to visit nearby scenic spots, and sometimes they traveled with other families.

It is another first in his life when he personally touched the white snow on the top of Mt. Rainier. Rainier Mountain National Park was named in 1899. At an elevation of 5,400 feet above sea level, the mountain is located in the southwest corner of the park, 11 miles from the park entrance.

The car was driven by his colleague Tseng. It would have been difficult for the boy to drive on the snowy mountain, especially since this was his first time seeing snow. In his whole life, he had never driven on a snowy road.

14.2.3 Visiting the world's largest private garden, Buchart Garden

In the summer of 1969, the boy drove his family to visit Buchart Garden. Starting at 8 o'clock in the morning, he drove northward across the border to British Columbia, Canada. It took about one and a half hour to reach Vancouver. Then they took the Port Angeles ferry barge, which was towed by a power boat to the opposite side of Victoria Island, and eventually he drove again awhile to get to the entrance of the garden.

The manicured lawns and trails link five major parks: sunken gardens, rose gardens, Japanese gardens, Italian gardens and Mediterranean gardens. Over 50 gardeners work hard all year to maintain the beauty of the place. Nearly one million plants bloom every year from March to October. In other months, visitors can see plants with bright berries on their branches, as well as carefully manicured shrubs and trees.

14.3 The second year of working at Boeing

14.3.1 Being transferred to the Boeing 747 cargo plane development

About 40 minutes from Seattle, there's a city called Everett, where the Boeing 747 Cargo Plane Department was located. He was transferred from the Boeing 757 New Aircraft Research and Development Department to here.

The Boeing 747 cargo plane was so built that the fuselage of the ordinary Boeing 747 passenger plane was elongated, and the engine power was increased. The boy was in the group of jet engine air inlet Cowl research: how to make the maximum amount of inlet air before take-off.

The work was studied by two groups of engineers: one group led by the boy, and the other group by a British engineer. Utilizing a water flow shape simulated an air flow shape called "water table." The supervisor was an American. He wanted to use the work of the British engineer, but the big boss preferred the boy's work.

"Is this the result of your experiment?" The big boss himself brought a set of black and white pictures of the water flow pattern to the boy's desk.

"Yes, that's the results of my research," he calmly answered.

"Can I adopt your research pictures?" the big boss said.

"Of course, that's my pleasure! I also hope that the results of my study could be adopted." As soon as he finished talking, the big boss walked away.

The United States has many immigrants and a company as big as Boeing had many as well. The experienced engineering staff had members from Germany, France, and Britain, advanced aircraft manufacturing countries.

14.4 The third year of working at Boeing

14.4.1 Almost becoming a research assistant for a professor

One day, after the boy and his professor discussed some courses, Professor Brown wanted him to be his research assistant, with another assistant called Fu Tong, to study the forest fire research project for Los Angeles County, which would pay half of his Boeing salary.

Also from Taiwan, Fu Tong had worked for this professor for five years. He had always been mistreated and not received a doctorate, even though he'd graduated from the top university in Taiwan, and in less than five years, how would it be possible for the boy to obtain a doctorate?

The boy did not want to repeat the results that Mr. Fu had suffered, so he refused the research assistant work offered by Professor Brown. On the other hand, the boy's major subject was gas dynamics, while his minor was heat transfer. These two subjects were in preparation for working in aerospace-related companies in the future.

14.4.2 Refusal to finish the doctoral thesis

The required courses for his doctoral degree would be completed soon. His advisor wanted to give the boy monthly research grants to start his doctoral thesis research.

If Professor Brown treated him the way his friend Fu had been treated, that would be unthinkable. Later, some students suggested that if he wanted to get his PhD, he should transfer to some another engineering related department.

Due to such kind of awkward condition, he stopped the continuing study, and tactfully refused the research scholarship to return to school full-time for his doctoral thesis research.

There were two options: either to quit school and become a businessman making good money, or to pursue a PhD and become a professor or a researcher. Eventually, he chose the former option, to become a businessman instead of an academic.

14.4.3 Going from Seattle to San Francisco for his new career

Fortunately, before going to San Francisco, he had gotten a job doing heat transfer work for a company called Bechtel Power Co. After his wife graduated from the University of Washington, he drove his family of three down to San Francisco to begin his new position, and after that he concentrated on his career development.

15 Bechtel Power Company employment and real estate investment

15.1 First day of employment in Bechtel Power Company

When the boy was still in Seattle, he asked a friend working in the Bechtel Power Co to turn in his resume. The next day he flew to their San Francisco headquarters for an interview. He was accepted immediately for employment, and was contracted to start work within two weeks.

The company was the largest in the United States specializing in the construction and design of nuclear power plants. He worked as a staff in the chief mechanical engineer office of mechanical engineering department.

He was in charge of the heat transfer analysis section, responsible for the heat transfer analysis and the design of the heating, ventilation and air conditioning (HVAC) systems.

After a few months, the mechanical engineering chief engineer Harry Smith summoned the boy. They wanted him to transfer to the chief engineer's office as a mechanical engineer specializing in heat transfer work. He said at the very beginning the group director Dwight Codington had already hired him and he didn't want to change his present situation, so he refused the request.

It was unbelievable that his heat-transfer expertise had made two executives scramble for it.

15.2 Reading a book was an incentive to invest in real estate

During lunchtime, he usually ate at an outside restaurant. The nearest restaurant was only five minutes away, while the farthest restaurant in Chinatown was 15 minutes. After lunch, he went to a nearby bookstore to stroll around and then came back to the office to work.

Once in the bookstore, he accidentally found a book titled "100 dollars to become 1 million dollars." He bought that book and read it at home over and over again. It described how to invest in real estate property: the point was either to buy an old property at a low price, renovate and then sell it, or rent it and wait for it to appreciate.

Although working at Bechtel, he took a real estate broker exam to get a license to buy a house for the investment. When his friends bought houses, he saved them money and got a small broker commission.

15.3 His first real estate investment

When he was working for Boeing in Seattle, he knew a hometown fellow who had bought a residential home and also invested in stocks.

Not only did he not buy any real estate, he also didn't play stocks.

At that time, Boeing laid off a lot of employees due to losing a bid for the Super-Sonic Transportation (SST) airplane. After he left Seattle, for a period of time the lawns in front of the houses along the whole streets were littered with for-sale signs. .

But when he got to San Francisco, he saved enough money from his salary to make a down payment on a house. He bought a 60-year-old house in the second Chinatown that had been built after the 1906 San Francisco earthquake. The small house had a bedroom, living room, bathroom, kitchen and basement.

The house that had been bought by his colleague from Bechtel (who had also come from Taiwan) in the suburbs was twice as expensive as the one that boy bought in the city.

15.4 The birth of Miss Daughter

In the second year of his employment at Bechtel, his wife gave birth to a daughter, who was born in the Tung Wah Hospital of Chinatown in San Francisco.

After she had stayed in the hospital for three days, a relative called Chiu Chie (who lived near Japan-town) came to her home to cook sesame oil chicken and oil rice for her to eat. It is a Taiwanese custom to cook these two items to nourish the new mother's body.

When a girl was born, it was the custom to give chocolates to colleagues and friends, while when a boy was born it was cigars. One month after the baby's birth, a party was held in the Golden Gate Park meadow, with about thirty relatives and friends attending.

15.5 His adoptive father came to the United States

In the spring of 1971, because of the adoptive mother's high blood pressure, she did not dare to fly in an airplane, and so the adoptive father came alone to the United States to visit the boy's family.

After the adoptive father arrived in the U.S.A., he was taken to a nearby sightseeing spot. Twice a week, while the boy was at work, his daughter-in-law took him and his grandson to buy their daily food in the first Chinatown.

Sometimes they bought their groceries and ate their lunch in the second Chinatown six blocks away. To drive to the first Chinatown took 15 minutes, while to walk to the second Chinatown only took 10 minutes.

Later in the Li-Yang museum in Golden Gate Park, his grandson attended the painting class, and the grandpa accompanied him every day. They went to the entrance of the Golden Gate Park only ten minutes away, but to see the scenery inside the whole park needed a whole day.

After two months, the boy took his whole family: adoptive father, wife, and son sightseeing. Driving nine hours a day, they took one month to travel around four states: California, Utah, Nevada, and Arizona.

The first sightseeing site was Salt Lake City in Utah. The lake water was frozen like ice cubes. The adopted father picked up a piece of lake ice to taste how salty it was, and then they went into the Mormon Church to see the large bronze pipe organ, and then the boy continued to drive south.

After they finished sightseeing in Salt Lake City, he drove southward continually to the **second sightseeing site** of Bryce Canyon. They enjoyed each layer of the mountain with the different colors of stone, and it looked like a castle. Then they stopped at the **third sightseeing site** in Arizona to see the Petrified Forest.

As far as you could see, there were trees that had fallen and petrified over millions of years. After they fell, they broke into small columns that were scattered on the ground. And then they drove to the **fourth sightseeing site** to see the colorful Painted Desert, where the sand on the small hill was dyed naturally in multi-colors.

The **fifth sightseeing site** was the Navajo American Indian Reservation District, where an American Indian tribe lived in the rocky caves of the desert. Just as in Taiwan's mountainous areas, there were many tribes living in their reserved area.

The **sixth sightseeing site** was the North Rim of the Grand Canyon. They stayed a cabin hotel during their stay. Normally tourists go first to the south rim, but they went to the north rim first to see the south rim scenery. The two rims of the landscapes are really very different, but the majestic mountains and the mystery of the valleys are incomparable.

The next day they stayed in the Grand Canyon for about two hours, and then left for Nevada.

Their seventh **sightseeing site** was the Hoover Dam, which at that time was the first and biggest concrete gravity arch-dam in the world.

They enjoyed the fantastic scenery at the great dam, with Mead Lake and the power generating stations at the bottom. They went to the visitors' center and bought some souvenirs. As the sun was going to drop into the ocean, they left and drove toward the eighth **sightseeing site,** Las Vegas, the world's biggest and beautiful gambling city.

Staying there a night, they checked out of their hotel the next morning and continued to Los Angeles, where he found a hotel near Disneyland, their **ninth sight-seeing site**. After they finished breakfast, they went to Disneyland.

That day was his daughter's birthday, so they celebrated it with a birthday party, playing in the park all day and all night. One of the most wonderful scenes was that both the boy and his 67-year-old adoptive father were riding on a sled, spearing through the false mountain cave at a high speed; rushing through the shallow water, which splashed them; and finally making them a little wet.

The next morning, after eating a hotel-supplied breakfast, they went home, driving along the 5th California mountain highway heading back to San Francisco.

15.6 When he returned to Taiwan, his adoptive father praised him

The Wen Chang park in Taoyuan downtown was a good place for the retired people to gather and chat. When his adoptive father was back in Taiwan, he talked to those retired elders about his sightseeing in the United States. He described the nine places they had visited.

They all envied his luck. The adoptive father had been treated such nice hospitality, and visited so many places most people couldn't do. He was admired for getting the chance to travel, and felt very happy and satisfied.

15.7 Buying a second house

The house in San Francisco, with 2,500 sq. ft., was really too small! On the weekend, to find a bigger house, the boy's family went to Newark, one hour drive to San Francisco. He found an American broker, local and most creditworthy, to show them a model house. The interior was well equipped with an answering machine beside the front door, a music system in the interior walls, and the patterned wallpapers were decorated on every room walls.

This last model home was not sold yet, and the price was pretty expensive because it was an exhibition house. There was no other choice, but they liked it, so they made an offer. The builder accepted it, and they bought that house. As for the house in San Francisco, it would be rented out. One day a colleague Wu, who also came from Taiwan, asked the boy on the telephone;

"I heard that you have bought another house recently," Wu asked,

"Yes! I've bought another house lately," he said.

"Then what about the house you're living in now?" Wu asked.

"I'm going to keep the house that I am still living in," he answered.

"Could you afford to pay the monthly installment?" Wu asked insolently.

"If I can't pay it, I'll sell it." Wu's tiresome questions were answered calmly by him.

It was no wonder Mr. Wu asked such a question, at that time, none of the colleagues came from Taiwan had bought a second house.

15.8 The birth of second son

The second son and daughter were born in the same city of San Francisco, but at different hospitals. The daughter was born at the Dong Hua Hospital in China town, while the second son at the Medical Hospital of University of California at San Francisco.

When the first two children were born, the boy did not take any leave, but this time, he took two weeks off, stayed at home in order to cook the sesame oil chicken and cared for them.

In a foreign country, relatives were scarce, friends were busy with their own things, and human relations were very weak, so everything had to be done by oneself.

15.9 Investing in a third house

The boy had moved four times in 10 years. When he lived in Newark, a builder in the next town of Union City had just started to construct new truck houses. In order to pre-buy a house in a better location, buyers lined up at 7 o'clock in the morning to select a house from the construction drawings.

After six months, when the second batch of house construction drawing came out, the price of second batch house had gone up 10% more than that of first batch. This was just enough for the round trip cost of his whole family to go back to Taiwan visiting.

15.10 Moving to a home with a swimming pool

One day, a house for sale sign was shown on the lawn that had a swimming pool in the backyard. The boy's family all liked it, and they bought the house because they wanted to enjoy the convenience of not going to the public swimming pool. But they found the pool was very troublesome.

To keep it clean was very time-consuming and tiresome. If they let autumn leaves get into it and did not clean it for a while, the water would turn yellow and dirty, and smell bad. In order to keep the swimming pool clean, it was very annoying.

Whenever the children wanted to swim, that boy had to sweep the leaves from the pool surface, clean the dirt and check the chlorine level; but after the cleaning, he was exhausted and could do nothing. But cleaning the swimming pool was worth for three children.

15.11 Unintentionally driving across a bridge from America to Canada

The first time, the boy was sent on a business trip to the Palisades nuclear power plant at Ann Arbor, Michigan. He had never been alone in the East, and he felt a little afraid, but the company had ordered it, the director's secretary had bought an airplane ticket for him, and he couldn't refuse to go.

The next day, he flew to the Detroit airport. After leaving the airport, he rented a car and checked the map. On driving to the power plant, he glimpsed a bridge with a special shape. It was not small, and looked like an old style antique bridge.

Driven by curiosity, he resolutely drove across the bridge. On the other side, he explored several streets, then tried to come back to the other end of the bridge, but there was a person standing there.

"Please show me your passport," the man asked.

"I don't have my passport with me. My company, Bechtel, sent me to Ann Arbor's Palisades Nuclear Power Plant on a business trip," he explained.

"Then do you have any company documents for me to see?" asked the man.

"Is it all right to show you a letter from my company?" The boy took a Bechtel letter from his briefcase and showed it to the man.

"Well, you can go!" The man looked at the company document and smiled.

It turned out that the bridge was to Canada, and the person was actually a customs officer. Because he didn't wear a uniform, it was hard to tell that he was a government official. The boy had traveled in Canada for ten minutes, shorter than the short-lived morning dews, and it was the world's shortest travel.

This was the first time that boy was on a business trip in America. It was so hard to believe that the customs facilities in both countries were so shabby. It was only as large as a guard house, but he didn't know whether it was renovated later. And then he hurried to the nuclear power plant.

15.12 Promoted to senior engineer

The Bechtel Power Company was contracted to design and build several nuclear power plants in different states at the same time.

The boy worked in the plant facilities special group, dedicated to designing six nuclear power plants at the same time. He designed the heating, ventilating, and air conditioning (HVAC) equipment in the plants, so that the staff could operate and maintain the proper temperature.

He worked so hard that he received praise from various project departments; therefore, after he had been working a few years in the company, he was promoted to senior engineer.

15.13 Investing in a six-unit apartment building

At that time, some engineers working in the company were enthusiastic about investing in real estate. One engineer from the Middle East who worked in the engineering department told the boy that he had a six-unit apartment for sale, and asked whether he wanted to buy it.

The apartment was located next to the Oakland airport in San Leandro. He took his wife to see it on the weekend, and the broker Milton Burke, who had handled a transaction for him once before, also arranged for him to buy this six-unit apartment complex.

Because the previous owner had not managed it properly, and was anxious to sell it, wanting to go back to his own country, the transaction went quickly. The parking lots outside the building had been renovated slightly, which raised the rent. When taking the Bay Area Rapid Transit (BART) train home from the company, a colleague named Guo, also from Taiwan, told the boy: "I heard you bought an apartment. I followed you and bought an apartment too."

"Why did you follow me to buy an apartment?" the boy asked Guo.

"Because the colleagues in our company said that if that boy bought a house, follow him to buy, and it will never be wrong," Guo told him in a contented way.

"Is there such a thing? You flatter me." The boy explained that, in fact, it was really a good time to invest in real estate.

15.14 Business trip to Pilgrim nuclear power plant

The Pilgrim nuclear power plant in Plymouth, Massachusetts had a problem with excessively high temperature at the top of the reactor and required the heat-transfer specialists from San Francisco headquarters to solve it.

Bill Frantino, who was in charge of the plant facility group leader in the Pilgrim project, requested the boy to accompany him to the job site to check the problem.

Originally they were ready to enter the reactor containment to check the high temperature spots, but after they went through the health test machine, neither of them were suitable to enter into the reactor containment.

Then the boy instructed the factory workers to measure the temperature above the insulation ring every two feet, and the results were as predicted: two spots of high temperatures were due to ripped-off insulation in the insulation ring.

The insulations in the high temperature portion were re-insulated after shutting down the whole power plant. It was the first time this had been discovered, and the boy's supervisor was delighted with his big discovery.

15.15 Moving in order to get a better school district

A portion of the population had emigrated from foreign countries to the United States. Especially in California, the majority of the inhabitants were from families that had immigrated to the United States from all over the world early and recently.

Although their respective reasons for coming to the United States were different, their aim was the same: to let their children get free education, and choose a good school district. So on the weekend the boy drove to Moraga, California.

While driving around the city of Moraga, he found a custom house was being built at the midway of a small hill: one-story, 4 bedrooms, 2 1/2 baths, a living room with cathedral ceiling, family room, kitchen, formal dining room, atrium, balcony attached to each bedroom, basement recreation room with a bar counter, two-car garage, shaggy roof, redwood siding, 200-foot-long private driveway on a half-acre land. The whole building was built with redwood, and it was completely different from an ordinary residential house.

The boy hired a broker, also from Taiwan, to write a purchase contract, and finally he bought this custom house. The city had Campolinglo High School, one of the 10 best high schools in America. When the new house was constructed completely, they moved for the third time in the Bay Area for the good school district.

15.16 Promoted to engineering expert after business trip to Turkey Point nuclear power plant

The specialist group in the last six months had added a subgroup called the start-up subgroup: all lines passing through the nuclear reactor building wall to the outside atmosphere must be pressure tested to prevent radiation leaking out.

The Turkey Point nuclear power plant, located 2 miles east of Homestead, Florida, needed this kind of test. The boy was sent to the job site to supervise the workers grinding the pipe-valves.

There were two groups of workers competing with each other; each group of three workers took turns grinding the valves. The group supervised by the boy ground six more pipe valves than the other group did, because he had supervised workers in Taiwan for six years.

He let the workmen grind the valve alone, because they did not like having somebody standing beside them and watching them. The boy went away to a quieter place to study for his engineer license test.

After each of them completed grinding a valve, the boy was asked to check the gauge pressure to see if it was high enough. The next day, the nuclear reactor containment was going to be pressurized, but the pressurizing operating engineer forgot to open one of the valves. He told a worker to open it, and the pressurization of containment was successful.

About two months after his business trip, the boy received a notice that he had passed the exam for a mechanical engineering license. At the same time, his supervisor gave him a raise and promoted him to an engineering specialist.

15.17 Attending summer class at Harvard University

In 1982, because the boy's oldest son, an 11th-grade high school student, had applied for a summer class at Harvard University, which was located in Cambridge, Massachusetts, the boy and his wife accompanied their son to the school for registration.

The three family menbers flew to Boston, rented a car, and drove to Harvard University in Cambridge. But before going to the school, he drove around Cambridge, enjoying seeing more than a hundred years of historical buildings. While the older son checked in with the registration office, he circled around the campus, and the buildings they saw were antique and impressive.

They reluctantly left the school and drove directly to Niagara Falls, which is located at the junction of New York State and Canada.

When they arrived at their destination, they saw Niagara Falls in Canada from the river shores of New York, and then from Canada they looked at the falls in the U.S.

The waterfall on either side looked a little different, but it was the same waterfall. The drop was 54 meters, and with the longest width in the world, it's an unparalleled sight, both thrilling and relaxing.

Wandering on the riverbank for a while, he drove along the highway in Canada; while enjoying the Canadian scenery, in the distance he could see the world's third highest tower, Skylon Tower.

After an hour or so, he returned to the United States, drove all the way to the Boston airport, and boarded the airplane back to San Francisco.

15.18 The broker fee was not reduced a dime

After having bought a house, he waited a while and then sold it for the sake of investment, making money from the house's appreciation. The broker normally obtained six percent of the house price as a broker fee. If the broker fee was reduced, he would not seriously look for a good house and obtain a good price for you.

One day that boy met a fellow who had also come from Taiwan. Originally the broker found a ten-unit apartment complex let him buy, but he offered to reduce the broker fees, and hence the broker helped the boy sell all the real property, trade up this apartment.

The boy never reduced the broker fee even a dime, and the broker naturally would find some ways to help him get a real benefit.

15.19 His picture was published in the Bechtel company's annual magazine.

The most excellent job for that boy in the Bechtel Company was the heat transfer analysis work. He was not only responsible for solving the heat transfer problems for six projects in the San Francisco headquarters, but also dealing with heat transfer problems in other branch offices.

If the branch office had a heat transfer problem, they sent the problem to the head office to solve the problem, and then sent the answers back to the branch office. Sometimes the boy would also go to the branch office to solve their problems. Once he was requested by the Houston branch office to go there for two months, where he analyzed the heat released out by the insulated electric wire for the whole plant.

In particular, for the insulation thickness of the heat pipe line in whole plant, he wrote a computer program to select the insulation thickness. The lesser amount of heat that was released, the more energy would be saved. The proper insulation saved a lot of energy, and energy saved was money saved.

Because of the insulation of pipelines, the loss of heat energy in the whole plant is minimized, and the economic benefits were really tremendous.

So John Smith, the director of the specialist group, asked for his permission to publish the theory of the insulation thickness for the hot pipeline in the Symposium of American Society of Mechanical Engineers.

In 1978, when the company's reporter visited Smith, the boy was also visited, and his photograph was taken and posted in the company's annual magazine reporting his special contribution.

In ASME meeting, his group director lectured on the theory and a computer program he had developed. The director wanted to be listed in the company's annual magazine, but did not make it; it required a true capability and wisdom to compete with colleagues in the workplace.

15.20 Sightseeing in the East with his son

That boy oldest son received four interview letters from different medical schools, three from schools in the East, and one in the West.

Wanting to travel, he accompanied his son to the three schools in the East for the medical school interviews. The father and son prepared their luggage and arrived at Washington Dulles Airport near dusk. They had reserved a hotel near Georgetown for two nights.

The next day, after breakfast, he drove to visit the interior of the White House, the Senate hall and the library. They also climbed to the top of the Statue of Liberty.

On the third day, his son went to Georgetown University Medical School for an interview, and then they flew immediately to New York City. They booked a hotel in the downtown area of New York City and prepared for sightseeing the next day.

He drove around New York City for the whole fourth day, including the World Trade Center on the 110 Twin Tower high rises, and visited the Wall Street Stock Market to see the stock clerk operating the stock. On the fifth day, after his son had his interview at New York University Medical School, they flew to the University of Massachusetts for the last interview.

Because last year, his oldest son had gone to the nearby Harvard University for Summer School, the surrounding scenic spots had already been visited, so they did not stay there too long before flying back to San Francisco.

15.21 Climbing up to the 110-story twin towers of the World Trade Center in New York

For sightseeing in New York City, the boy took the opportunity of accompanying his older son to a medical school interview.

The World Trade Center was a large complex of seven buildings, containing the two tallest buildings which were called World Trade Center Twin Towers. Both were 110 floors, and 417 and 415 meters tall, respectively. The boy took the elevator to the observatory deck to see the panoramic view of New York City.

At that time, it was the tallest building in the world. The World Trade Center was destroyed during the September 11 attacks.

15.22 Four parents came to America to be entertained by their children

In the summer of 1986, the boy's father-in-law had just retired from the government office, so the parents of two families came to the United States and were entertained by their children.

Thinking about 14 years ago, the adoptive father came to the United States to visit the boy's family. At that time they had been living in their first, very small, old house (the lot size = 1,000 square feet, 1 acre = 43,560 square feet).

In recent years, dealing with the real estate, he had bought a huge house on the middle of a hill, which was a custom-built new building on about a half-acre land (lot size = 22 times bigger than the first house).

The house included 4 bedrooms, a living room, a family room, 2 1/2 bathrooms and a recreation room with a bar, for a total of 2,700 sq. ft. of living quarter, using all redwood to build the custom-made house.

When he had been poor in Taiwan, the boy had been looked down on by others. But now he could compete professionally with American colleagues in the company, and they respected and admired each other. The happiest thing was that he had a comfortable house where their four parents could stay.

They were first entertained by visiting places of interest near the Bay Area and then drove to the Lake Tahoe, which is located on a high mountain. The group of two families took a cruise boat to see the lake's surrounding scenery, and later beside the lakeshore, their group picture was taken by a professional photographer.

Lake Tahoe actually belongs to two states. On the lake map if a line is drawn vertically down in the middle, the left side belongs to California, while the right side to Nevada. Casinos were banned in California, but not on the Nevada side, so they had to go to the Nevada side whenever they wanted to visit the casino.

Early the next morning, they went to a restaurant beside the lake. While they were eating breakfast, they appreciated the lake view. When the sun was out, the lake appeared three colors: from the lake shore to the center of the lake there was light green, green, and dark blue in layers.

When they left, they spent one hour driving around the lake, and then they drove another three and half hours back to the Moraga house on the outskirts of San Francisco.

The second week, the boy asked the company for two days off, so that, with the two weekend days, they could have a total of four days to drive to the Grand Canyon.

Starting at seven o'clock that Saturday morning, he stopped wherever they found a scenic spot along the way. When they were close to the Grand Canyon, they chose a hotel in Phoenix, stayed one night and drove to the Grand Canyon the next day.

They arrived at the Canyon Village store, bought some souvenirs and then went to the mountain top of the canyon. Only the adoptive father followed the boy to the observatory platform to see the Grand Canyon panorama and look down to the valley village. His adoptive father said the people seemed to be as small as ants. The Grand Canyon was so spectacular that the four parents were amazed.

After leaving the Grand Canyon, they spent a night in Las Vegas, ate dinner in the restaurant beside Las Vegas Boulevard, watched the casino's twinkling colorful lights, and this was the most beautiful night street scenery in the world.

The next morning, they hover about the Las Vegas Boulevard to see the daytime street scenery. The small statues in front of each casino were the shrunken versions of world famous scenic buildings such as Triumph, Pyramid, Statue of Liberty, and so on.

There were fascinating paintings on the ceiling and walls inside the casino, which looked like the drawings of

Michelangelo, who was the most famous painter, sculptor and architect in the world. They went in the casino to visit the facilities inside and then he drove the whole family back to their home in the Bay Area.

The four parents' visas were only good for one month. He arranged for them to visit Los Angeles a week before they had to leave the country.

Along the 101 Interstate, the four parents sat in the car, enjoying the ocean view on the right side and the mountain scenery on the left. However, this ocean shore road was more rugged than the mountain side road, so he drove slower because there were a lot of turns.

When they arrived at the hotel near Disneyland, the sun was close to the horizon, so they quickly booked a hotel. Early next morning, after breakfast, he bought tickets to go into the park. He offered to rent two wheelchairs for the mothers to sit in, but his mother-in-law said she was still so young that she had no need for a wheelchair.

As a result, only the adoptive mother was in the wheelchair, and her daughter-in-law pushed her to see all the activities in the park. And they could only watch some programs, but not participate in activities.

But they all felt fresh and interested in every show, because there was still no such thing in Taiwan at that time, and especially no panoramic round movie screen (360-degree).

In order to record the visit of the four parents to the United States, the boy bought a video recorder, and recorded

several video tapes. The parents brought a video pro-
jector and took those recorded tapes back to Taiwan for
relatives and friends to watch.

At that time it was unusual to travel from Taiwan to a
foreign country. They considered themselves lucky to
be able to enjoy this in their lifetime. Everybody wants
their parents to be satisfied and happy, but the methods
are quite different.

15.23 Invitation letter from registered world celebrities

One day in 1992, when the boy came home, he checked
his mailbox and found that the organizer of the "Who's
Who Worldwide" had sent an invitation letter to him.

The next day, when he went to the office, he called the
organizer and asked for details. If somebody wanted to
log into the celebrity record, a plaque and a register book
would be given. Both items cost money, but since the
plaque cost less, he selected that for memory.

The plaque read: MEMBERSHIPS ARE LIMITED TO
INDIVIDUALS WHO HAVE DEMONSTRATED
LEADERSHIP AND ACHIEVEMENTS IN THEIR
OCCUPATION, INDUSTRY OR PROFESSION

1992 Platinum Edition of the Who's Who Worldwide

15.24 Riding on a small traffic airplane to work for the nuclear power plant

The P G & E utility company had several small commuter airplane for their employees in the remote main office, but these small private aircraft could only carry four to six passengers. This company owned the Diablo Canyon Nuclear Power Plant, which was located on the shore at San Luis Obispo in northern San Francisco.

He was requested to solve the heat transfer problem in that plant.

When he arrived at the plant, which was just running, each employee entering the plant was required to wear a badge measuring the degree of radiation exposure.

He had investigated why the temperature beside some of the machines was so high, and he stayed inside about half an hour measuring the temperature. After coming out from the plant, he hurriedly boarded a small plane back to San Francisco.

15.25 Resigning because he was unwilling to work at the New Jersey nuclear power plant

One morning in 1992, that boy's boss wanted to send him to the East, to work at the New Jersey Nuclear Power Plant for two years. Although he could fly back to the San Francisco head office once a month, he considered that he had real estate that he needed to manage himself. Returning once a month would not be enough to take care of his own business.

So he simply tendered his resignation and returned to Taiwan for a year's vacation. He went to see places he had never been able to visit previously due to being in school or working in the factory.

15.26 A sightseeing trip to eight countries in Western Europe

More than 26 years ago, there were only two travel agents in the Bay Area. Now, with increased yearly Asian immigrants and foreign students, there are often one or two travel agencies in one supermarket.

Western Europe had a total of 13 countries. The boy and his wife had traveled to all of them except five: Spain, Portugal, Ireland, Luxembourg, and Andorra.

Of those 13 countries, with the exception of the British and Irish islands, the other 11 countries are all connected together. Some of the countries are small enough that one could drive through two or three of them in one day.

When entering the border, the tour guide collected passports to let the customs officers to stamp entry visas; when leaving the border, they got exit stamps. So a total of 16 visa seals were stamped at the end of the trip.

15.27 The parents-in-law came to America again to visit Yellowstone Park

After that boy's parents and his wife's parents had visited the United State, the latter were still interest in coming for sightseeing again. Of course, that boy couldn't refuse them when they wanted to come.

On the second day of their arriving, the boy's wife called the travel agency, and the four persons: his parents-in-law, his wife and he went to tour the Yellowstone Park. The park was founded in 1872 and is one of the largest national parks in the United States.

The park has geysers, hot springs, fumaroles and mud pots, and is really a fascinating place. The legendary wildlife includes grizzly bears, wolves and herds of bison and elk. More than half of the world's geysers are found in Yellowstone, and Old Faithful was one of the largest geysers, so it was worth seeing its eruption. Because of the group tour, the tour leader took all the members to visit many beautiful natural wonders that they had never seen before.

15.28 The son receives admission notices from two medical schools

After finishing three interviews by medical schools in the East, the boy's son was interviewed by the forth medical school of the University of Southern California two weeks later. And after another week, the boy's son and his family were delighted to obtain an acceptance letter from the Massachusetts Medical School.

Originally his son was planning to go to the Massachusetts medical school, but a week later, the Southern California medical school also sent a letter of acceptance to his son, who immediately decided to accept the Southern California admission.

He had been born in L.A. and liked the weather in California, but the most important reason was that after graduation, it was easier for a local intern doctor to be employed in California hospitals. Sure enough, he's now a physician at a hospital in Los Angeles.

15.29 The company group director prepares cocktails for the employees at the Christmas party

There was a special group of the mechanical engineering department in the Bechtel company, called the Plant Facility Specialty Group, including six subgroups: Heat Transfer, Nuclear Radiation, Control Valves, Fire Protection, Power Plant Start-up, and Factory Crane. A group director was in charge of these six subgroups; each subgroup was led by six subgroup directors, and the boy was responsible for the Heat Transfer subgroup.

When Russell Brown was the group director, every year the boy went to his home to celebrate Christmas Day. Every year when Christmas came, the six subgroup directors took their families to the party. The meal was brought in from an outside vendor, everybody stood or sat on the sofa to chat and drink; and waitresses brought the food to let everybody pick up what they wanted.

In particular, the group director stood in front of his bar to mix drinks for his subordinates and their dependents. It was rare to see a boss entertain his subordinates with such zeal.

16 Caesar Engineering Company and Cigna

16.1 Two companies working in joint operations

After quitting his previous job, from the newspaper the boy found a company was seeking engineers in Oakland, which was located on the other end of the Bay Bridge. The interview was at the Caesar Engineering Company, but Cigna hired him. It turned out that these two companies were engaged in the nuclear waste disposal project of the Idaho nuclear waste plant.

As a result, the chief engineer of Cigna got him to be the group head of heat transfer and heating, ventilating, and air conditioning (HVAC) section, and gave him a fairly large office to use. Not surprisingly, two companies had fought each other to hire the boy.

After about two years, due to his health and his apartment business, he tendered his resignation to the company. Running his own real estate business was less pressure and gave him relaxed semi-retirement work.

16.2 Applying for a new apartment balcony construction permission using a mechanical engineer's license

When the balcony of the apartment had to be renovated, it required a licensed constructor to apply for a permit from the city government, but that boy used his own engineering license to apply for the permit.

He then hired a non-licensed experienced contractor from Taiwan and a local temporary worker to renovate the balcony, but the material such as wood and cement were provided by him. By contracting this way saved he about half of the cost.

He also bought the tools that the workers needed; hence after certain period of time he had accumulated so many tools that it looked like the tools belonged to a small factory.

16.3 Going back to Taiwan and attending the Taipei Institute of Technology alumni reunion

As soon as the boy went back to home town, there was a classmate reunion. This was the first time a reunion was held in the Bei Tou Grand Hotel. They were all seated on two ten-seat round tables, listening to Taiwanese folk songs sung by some live singers.

When he went back to Taiwan, he also visited some factories that had been opened or worked by his classmates: Wang had opened a welding rod factory; Lin had opened a pressing products factory; and Fang was employed in a nuclear power plant. After visiting his classmate Huang's workplace, the South Asia Plastic factory, Huang brought him to the Taiwan fertilizer factory in Sin Tsu, and their classmate Jiang treated them to lunch inside the factory. When his classmate Kao was still alive, he visited Kao's touring car seat factory.

16.4 Observing the stars of the universe at the observatory

At Oakland Hill, about 50 miles away from the boy's house, was Chabot Space and Sciences Center. During the day, you could see the universe's stars simulated inside the building, and at night you could observe the actual planets and constellations outdoors.

On one occasion, the boy saw Saturn with its outer ring of discs. It seemed to be the size of a basketball and was very wonderful. He was very excited to see a planet other than Earth.

Although his son had given him an eight-inch telescope for his birthday, living in the city surrounded by high buildings, he could only see the stars in a limited area of the sky; therefore, this telescope was hardly used. He studied astronomy by reading astronomy magazines, watching the sky on a website for more than ten years, and could be dubbed an amateur astronomer.

16.5 Returning to Taiwan and visiting the Taiwan Power Company Chairman Chen Lan kao

When the boy lived in the Bay Area, for the sake of helping his children learn Mandarin, he established jointly a Chinese school with some other Chinese. When a parent surnamed Chen heard that he was going back to Taiwan for a visit, he was asked to bring a letter to Mr. Chen Lan Kao, a chairman of the Taiwan Power Company.

After returning to Taiwan, his classmate Wang asked his driver to take him to the Taiwan Power Building, and he gave the letter to Chairman Chen. Both of the Chens, one in the U.S. and one in Taiwan, were Cantonese-speaking and from the same hometown. The boy talked with the chairman about the economic utilization of nuclear power for about one hour, and then he left the Taiwan Power Building.

16.6 Being welcomed by his classmates Mr. and Mrs. Song

When he returned to Taiwan, he visited Mr. and Mrs. Song, both of them were his classmates. When they went to the east of New York to visit their daughters, on the way back to Taiwan they came to the west of San Francisco to visit the boy.

After everyone had greeted each other in the office of Song's own company, Mrs. Song brought both the boy and his wife to visit their expansive new house just bought recently. After the visit, they served a meal in the top restaurant in Taipei. Here the boy and his wife once again thank them for their sincere hospitality, although classmates Song were not in this world anymore.

17 A semi-retired status to travel

17.1 Experience on apartment management

With his former experience as a chairman of a company and over forty years of experience in apartment management, the boy had been working as a consultant for a friend's apartment complex.

Generally, the apartment management and maintenance were separated into two departments: the management people would not do the repair work, and the maintenance people would not do the management work, but the boy had both kinds of experiences.

Apartment investment in the United States was a kind of enterprise, called the apartment investment industry. Actually the apartment was rented to these kinds of people: the school's newly-graduated students, new employees from other cities, immigrants just coming from foreign countries, and those without enough money to buy a house.

17.2 Traveling in the Hawaiian islands

Because the boy's daughter lived in Honolulu for six years, the boy and his wife also went there to visit her five or six times. And they visited one or two islands each time.

Hawaii has four large islands: Hawaii, Oahu, Maui, and Kauai. Since Oahu's Honolulu is the Hawaiian Islands' commercial, political, cultural, and tourist center, the transportation to each island was mainly aviation.

Over the last several years, due to problems with arthritis, every year the boy and his wife went to Hawaii to escape the cold humid weather once or twice during the winter season. The highest daily temperature was 78 degrees Fahrenheit, while the lowest is 68 degrees in January. If possible, the boy and his wife would like to retire in a retirement center in the Hawaiian Islands.

17.3 No chemical therapy was needed to escape the jaws of death after colon cancer surgery

The American Cancer Society indicated that bowel bleeding might be a symptom of colorectal cancer. The boy thought that it could be the recurrence of hemorrhoids surgery from ten years prior, and hence did not pay special attention.

It was later decided to go to the internal clinic for a colonoscopy. Based on the colonoscopy, the doctor announced that he had colon cancer. he was alarmed, thinking that the end of the world had arrived, and only one way to survive continually was to remove the polyps away as soon as possible.

On the middle of his belly, the surgeon made a vertical cut a foot long, and due to the success of the surgery he escaped from death's door.

The large intestine was cut off 10 inches and connected with two plastic couplings: one on the ascending large intestine in the right and the other on the S-shaped large intestine in the left. He was discharged after eight days of hospitalization in a first-class single ward.

That boy was very lucky: in the ascending large intestine, polyps have been up to two-thirds the diameter of the large intestine, so they cut off 6 inches, and when the s-shaped part of the large intestine was full of polyps, they cut off 4 inches. The intestine walls of the cut part of the large intestine had no cancer, so there was no need for chemotherapy, even without taking medicine.

Thereafter, every two or three years, the large intestine was inspected through a colonoscopy. Every time, there were two or three small polyps which were removed by electric heating, and he has survived fifteen years until now. He later explored why no aggressive cells had spread to the colon, rectum glands, and lymph. The reason was that when he had been employed by the Bechtel Company 32 years before, he started to drink two or three cups of coffee every weekday and ate a daily diet of green vegetables. Later in the newspapers and magazines there was an article that said drinking coffee has an anti-cancer effect..

17.4 The luxury cruise along the Alaska bay

He took a plane from San Francisco to Anchorage, Alaska, then transferred to the Island Princess Ship for a luxury cruise along the Alaska bays to see snow-white glaciers and icebergs.

They disembarked at three of Alaska's most fascinating towns: Skagway, Juneau and Ketchikan, and the couple enjoyed the local scenery, along with the spectacular Glacier Bay National Park. It was different from the sightseeing bus because there was no need to move luggage out of the cruise ship at the different locations. Eventually, the cruise ship sailed to Seattle and they flew back to San Francisco.

17.5 On the experience of apartment maintenance

The boy was able to repair the whole house, except for the roof, the carpet and the refrigerator. He painted the inside and outside of the houses, repaired or changed the equipment and appliances inside the house by himself. He not only instructed the outside technical worker to do the repair work, but also was a maintenance teacher: choosing a worker among the tenants who was willing to learn to do the repairs, he paid them, and instructed them as well as supervising them step-by-step.

17.6 Vacation at the leisure ranch

In the northern part of California, south of the Oregon border, there is a small village called Hornbook, which only has one street. On both sides of the street, there is a post office, a couple of restaurants, and a grocery store. About 20 houses are located behind both sides of the street; and south of the village, there is a leisure ranch named R-Ranch.

Covering about 5,000 acres, the ranch had more than 80 horses, two swimming pools, two tennis courts, two fishing ponds, flat houses with more than 40 bedrooms, more than 20 wooden huts, a group of shooting ranges, and many hunting areas.

This ranch belonged to 2,500 shareholders, and the owners called each other "pardner" rather than partner. More than 40 years ago, the boy had bought a share of about two and a half acres, but the land was not demarcated, and he did not know exactly which piece belonged to him, but anyway, all of the facilities inside were shared between the shareholders. There was full-time staff in the field to deal with everyday things.

The Gate of Leisure Fame (R-RANCH)

When the children were in middle high school, the boy had a van which contained a small hexagonal table. He could drive it to the river side of the ranch for camping and they could barbecue and fish at the same time. The river, called Klamath River, flowed from the southern Oregon to the northern California and then turn left into the Pacific Ocean.

The river was rich in salmon. There was a fish hatchery raising small fish to put into the river, then the small fish swam downstream to the Pacific Ocean to grow into big fish, and from downstream the female fish swam upstream to the hatchery. When a concrete dike was built on the river, the female fish would fly over the dike to go upstream, so the fish either flew over or died.

The stables were quite busy, and the pardner who wanted to ride a horse was required to register one day ahead. No experience was required for riding, because these horses were trained and very obedient. When riding on

The boy, his son and daughter riding horses

the trail, there was a trainer on the first horse, and the others followed one by one in a line.

On the returning trail, almost at the end, they gave the horse one kick in the belly, and the horse began trotting. Then they kicked one more time, and the horse started galloping. But the boy did not dare to kick a third time, lest he would be thrown to the ground. It was a pleasure to ride a horse for the first time in his life! The young guys rode much faster than their father.

After having dinner at the restaurant in the evening, the farm held a tournament, with a trophy for whoever won. When they woke up in the morning they could see the sunrise, because the ranch was located in a basin surrounded by mountains, and the sun shone on the whole ranch.

After watching the sunrise, they ate breakfast at the fast food restaurant next to the swimming pool, and then the children swam in the pool. The next day, the sun had not yet risen when the children's mother drove them to the fishing pond specially dug for the children. They fished quite a lot but threw the small fishes back into the pond.

When the parents of the boy's wife came to visit the United States, they also visited the quiet leisure life of the American ranch.

During night time, there were no clouds, only the round, bright moon, but the whole sky was full of twinkling, diamond-like stars. Because in the suburbs the sky was free from air and light pollution, the whole sky looked lower than in the city, and as if the hands could reach out to pluck down the stars.

The boy's two sons and daughter fishing

Because of the rotation of the earth around the sun, every hour the position of each constellation also changed accordingly; and during the spring, summer, autumn, and winter seasons, the constellation was not in the same location.

Astronomers divided the entire sky into 88 constellations, which are zoned on the model "celestial globe." The boy had a "celestial globe" that he kept at home, and it is printed below.

Celestial Globe
The surface of the Celestial Globe included countless stars of different brightness, the Milky Way, countless galaxies, countless nebulae, and 88 constellations, and covered the whole Earth.

Late at night, it could be seen that twelve constellations crossed a white Milky Way; the former was also called the "Zodiac" and the latter the "Galaxy." He used the star map to identify each constellation. All the facilities and natural surroundings of the farm were fully enjoyed, but hunting was really prohibitive to him. If you didn't kill the beast, it would bite you in turn.

If Americans were on vacation, they didn't carry any cell phone or answer any phone calls, and in this way, they could absolutely isolate themselves from the busy world to be completely relaxed.

17.7 Who was the originator of the adoption deal?

His adoptive mother had eight sworn sisters, and every year they had a dinner together, and that boy was always taken to attend. When he was still in the 13 years of secrecy period, the adoptive mother never said that the eldest sworn sister was the elder sister of his biological father that means the eldest sister was his "aunt".

After the 13 years of secrecy were over, the other relatives have been readjusted to their correct relation, but the relation with his aunt was still mysterious and not clear, and from the inference, it was not difficult to judge that the great aunt of the sworn sister should be that boy's aunt, because she was the elder sister of his biological father.

Twenty years ago, when he went back to visit Taiwan, the sworn sister's son, who was called "Aha-ye," came to visit him, only said a few words, and then left, apparently feeling embarrassed. If the aunt did not handle this deal with conspiracy, that boy wouldn't be adopted.

17.8 Three turning points in his successful life

These are the three turning points that made that boy's achievements in his successful life:

The first turning point: getting into the Taipei Institute of Technology was a major turning point. If he had not passed the test, he wouldn't have been able to continue to study, and only to be a lifetime worker. This was how his fate changed from no opportunity to study into having a chance to study.

The second turning point: when working in the Petroleum Company of Taiwan, he was lucky to get advice from a colleague and applied for a full scholarship to study in an American graduate school, so that poor people could have a chance to study abroad. This was the promotion of his education from one country's system to jump into the international community.

The third turning point: becoming an apartment manager by chance. When he was the manager of an apartment building, he was dreaming of buying apartments by saving money from his future salary. Accordingly, 20 years later, this dream was fulfilled. This was his discovery of enterprise, from the working class to step into the business world.

Afterword

Although the boy was born to be adopted, before he was 13 years old, he thought, like other children, that the adoptive parents were his biological parents. He didn't know that he was adopted.

In fact, the adoptive parents did take him as their own born son, although in his youth time, the foster parents wanted him to help families: after school they made him do work, such as watering vegetables, being a hawker and a coolie, and in this way, trained him to be hard-working.

Because of hardship, he cultivated diligent reading habits to make himself smarter, and to think in a more advanced way. Though he had no money, he wanted to study abroad in the future, and fortunately he obtained a full scholarship to study in the United States.

It was most important that in his still hours, the adoptive father inculcated him, encouraged him, and expected him to be successful.

If there was no adoptive father's love, there was no boy today, and his adoptive father was really very great!

After coming to the United States, he struggled with full-time studying while part-time working; and finally gained economic stability in the U.S.A. He had good employment after graduation, retired from Bechtel Power

Company as an engineering specialist, and invested in real estate from his salary savings.

The boy's living style was low-key, taking the middle way, and being content. People's happiness neither necessarily depends on their authority, high or low, nor on the accumulation of wealth, more or less, but true happiness really relies on health and contentment.

People live in the world, and most people say that they suffer hardship, but they understand suffering differently. For decades, human beings live as if they are acting on a stage.

What kind of role, the director of the designated; the fate of the doomed; everyone has no choice. After the play is over, you bow down off the stage. From the planet of Earth, you disappear into the vast universe, and nothing else is known.

So the world is worldly, and nothing is worth disputing. This has described the poor guy walking back to 83 years of the tunnel of time. His personal real life, the experience of a lifetime, and the journey through the road of hardship has been recorded in the genre of fiction.

The story of this poor guy proves that to get a good harvest, no matter what other people do, as long as you "take hardship" and "take diligent." This is what Americans say: "No pain, no gain"! This is a good example to be used as a reference for others.

He lived through three different eras: Japanese, Chinese, and the United States. Every human being is born into this world, grows up, and must find some kind of work to support themselves, except those who are born into a rich family, and can go through life without doing any work at all. This is called fate. A different fate brings different experiences. It does no good to complain.

Finally, thanks to my family, relatives, and friends for giving the author valuable advice and supports during in the process of writing!

Yang, Chin Sheng
California, U.S.A.
February 25, 2019

Author's Brief Biography

Chin Sheng Yang
(楊金盛)

The author was an early foreign student from Taiwan to the United States for the advanced study. After finishing the studies, he was employed by three large companies: Boeing, Bechtel Power Company, and Kaiser Engineering Corporation.

Experiences and awards:
Retired as an engineering specialist
- California Licensed Professional Mechanical Engineer ... PE
- Awarded in the "Who's Who Worldwide"
- Praised in 1978 annual magazine of Bechtel Power Company
- Published a book written in Chinese language

Hobbies: Jogging, Listening to Music, Traveling, Amateur Astronomer

Schools graduated:
1955   Taiwan Taipei Institute of Technology (5 year courses) Diploma
1963   University of California at Los Angeles (UCLA) BSME
1967   University of Southern California (USC) MSME

The author

Chin Sheng Yang was born in Taiwan and adopted
at birth by a mason and his family. Growing up in
poverty around the time of World War II, he did
what he could to help his family survive, working
as a peddler selling vegetables and candy on the
street and a coolie, carrying bricks for his adopted
father's masonry projects, while also working hard
at his studies to improve his circumstances. When
he was offered a scholarship to study in the United
States, he moved to California to further his education. Attending UCLA and USC while working at
night, he made a name for himself as an engineer,
eventually working at Boeing in Seattle and later
Bechtel in the Bay Area. He managed, through
hard work and determination, to build a successful career and develop an impressive real estate
investment portfolio, raising his situation from a
childhood of poverty to a prosperous and successful life in America for himself and his family.

The publisher

*He who stops
getting better
stops being good.*

This is the motto of novum publishing, and our focus
is on finding new manuscripts, publishing them and
offering long-term support to the authors.
Our publishing house was founded in 1997, and since
then it has become THE expert for new authors and
has won numerous awards.

**Our editorial team will peruse each manuscript
within a few weeks free of charge and without
obligation.**

You will find more information about
novum publishing and our books on the internet:

w w w . n o v u m p u b l i s h i n g . c o m

www.ingramcontent.com/pod-product-compliance
Lightning Source LLC
Chambersburg PA
CBHW060310100426
42812CB00003B/726